Dec 2002

FOOD FOR FRIENDS

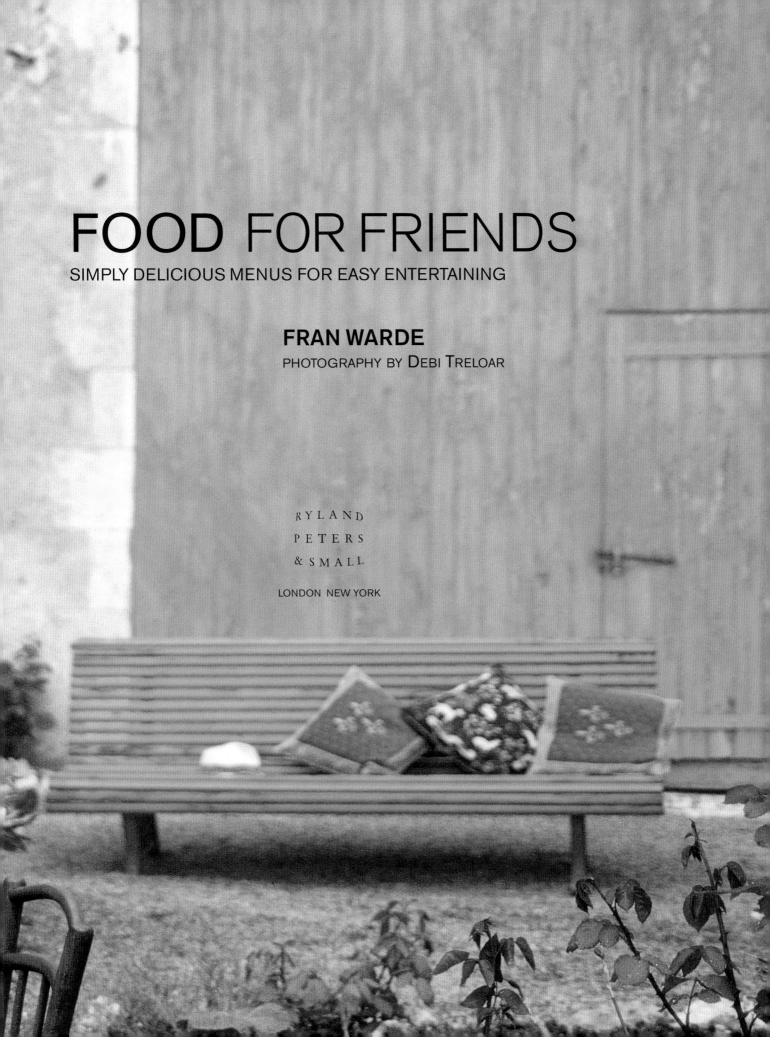

FOOD FOR FRIENDS

SIMPLY DELICIOUS MENUS FOR EASY ENTERTAINING

FRAN WARDE

PHOTOGRAPHY BY DEBI TRELOAR

RYLAND
PETERS
& SMALL

LONDON NEW YORK

First published in the United States in 2002
by Ryland Peters & Small, Inc.
519 Broadway, 5th Floor
New York, NY 10012
www.rylandpeters.com

10 9 8 7 6 5 4 3 2 1

Text © Fran Warde 2002
Design and photographs
© Ryland Peters & Small 2002

Library of Congress Cataloging-in-Publication Data
Warde, Fran.
  Food for friends : simply delicious menus for
easy entertaining / by Fran Warde.
    p. cm.
  ISBN 1-84172-278-2
    1. Cookery, International. 2. Entertaining. 3. Menus.
  I. Title.
  TX725.A1 W33 2002
  642'.4–dc21   2001048831

Printed and bound in China

Senior Designer
Paul Tilby

Editors
Elsa Petersen-Schepelern
Sally Somers
Jennifer Herman

Location Research
Kate Brunt
Sarah Hepworth

Production
Patricia Harrington

Art Director
Gabriella Le Grazie

Publishing Director
Alison Starling

Food Stylist
Fran Warde

Props Stylist
Emily Chalmers

Indexer
Hilary Bird

Dedication
To my Boys, big and little

NOTES

All spoon measurements are level unless
specified otherwise.

Ovens should be preheated to the specified
temperature.

If using a convection oven, cooking times should
be reduced according to the manufacturer's
instructions.

Speciality Asian ingredients are available in larger
supermarkets and Asian stores.

Several recipes in this book use self-rising
flour. If unavailable, use all-purpose flour plus
extra baking powder in the ratio of 2 teaspoons
baking powder to each 1 3/4 cups flour.

contents

secrets of easy entertaining

Food and friends go hand in hand, but how many times have we had people coming over for a meal and panicked that we don't know what to make? It doesn't matter how good a cook you are, we all need some inspiration from time to time. When cooking for friends, remember the most important thing is that they came over to talk to you, not to test your cooking skills. Keep it simple, get organized, and everything will go smoothly. Choose recipes you know you can manage in your kitchen, with ingredients you know you can find. Read the recipes through before you start, refer to the work plan, then just relax and enjoy the shopping and cooking.

Simplicity is important. Many people have just a handful of recipes they like to cook, but if those dishes work and are a pleasure to eat, then no one will mind being served the same thing on more than one occasion.

Don't be afraid to cut corners in your kitchen. If you are short of time or energy, buy olives and thinly sliced prosciutto or salami from a good gourmet store. Serve them with crusty bread and good olive oil, and everyone will be happy. Then you just have to cook one course— entrée or dessert—and buy the other. You can find delicious fruit tarts from pâtisseries, fresh figs or melons with finely sliced prosciutto, or stuffed pastas and sauces. Don't be ashamed to buy some of the food— good cooking starts with the shopping!

Shop and cook—yes, entertaining is as simple as that.

I like to shop from small traders. Their produce is less likely to be mass-produced and transported unnecessary distances, and will taste better for it, I promise you. It can be more expensive, but it's really worth it, for quality as well as to lend support to small, local producers.

I find that choosing a style is important as it can add a little extra drama and beauty to the meal. You can take it as far as you wish: you'll find it's fun to vary the traditional presentation with everyone sitting around the table with the same food and uniform look. Be bold. This doesn't mean buying a whole new set of china—it's about adding your own touches; napkins tied with herbs, bamboo stalks as flowers, or just petals and candles floating in a large shallow dish. Add glitter to the flower water, put pebbles on the table to create that seaside look, use shells for individual salt and pepper holders, cut out squares of brightly colored paper to make place mats, use a length of beautiful fabric as a runner up the middle of the table—the list is endless. Set your artistic side free!

When all the cooking is under control, set the table sooner rather than later, because it's not something you want to do at the last minute. From then on, it's down to the handy Work Plan alongside each menu to help you arrive smoothly at a delicious meal on the table.

I really want you to enjoy your kitchen and your cooking. It's great to go out, but some of the most memorable and enjoyable times will be in the comfort of your own home in relaxed company. If you have bought this book, you obviously have an interest in cooking, either as a beginner or an experienced cook with flair and creativity. So just turn the pages, choose the occasion, and create your menu from the suggestions given. Shop and cook—yes, it's as simple as that. Oh, and don't forget to pour a drink, put on some music, and enjoy your cooking.

tips and hints

Cooking is one of life's pleasures and it can really bring joy to a home. Cooking a good meal binds the love and friendship between family and friends, and helps create warm and kind memories. Entertaining needn't be daunting.

EASY ENTERTAINING

MAKE IT EASY ON YOURSELF

• If cooking is not your strong point, don't despair. Choose easy recipes and menus that won't challenge your skills—slowly your courage will grow and everyone will be amazed at your new-found talents. Don't be put off and remember that practice makes perfect.

PLANNING MENUS

• You will find menus that have been planned for you. They are designed to help with the first stumbling block of deciding what to serve. Sometimes there are a few choices, but most menus comprise balanced ideas without repetitive flavors, and tastes and textures that will complement each other.

KITCHEN EQUIPMENT

• As soon as you have chosen the menu, check that you have all the necessary kitchen equipment. If not—buy, borrow, or improvise.

SHOPPING LISTS

• It sounds obvious, but make a list. I find it easiest to separate the items into fish/meat, vegetables/fruit, groceries, and drinks. Shop for dry goods in advance and buy the perishables on the day of the party.

PLAN YOUR WORK

• Look at the Work Plan for each menu and make anything that can be cooked in advance. Chill the drinks the night before and open red wine an hour or two before serving: this lets it breathe so the flavors will improve and develop.

SET THE SCENE

• Set the table as far in advance as possible and set up any special little table details, such as place cards, vases, napkins, candles, or tea lights.

BUY THE BEST INGREDIENTS

• Buy the best you can afford. Think "Quality not Quantity."

• Buy the freshest, best-looking food—you will taste the difference.

THE BEST FLAVORS

• Invest in a good pepper mill—freshly ground black pepper is by far the best.

• I prefer sea salt, though kosher salt is also good.

• A useful tip for juicing limes and even lemons is to microwave them on HIGH for 40 seconds, or warm them in hot water—either method makes juicing a lot easier.

• Serve salads at room temperature to let the flavors come through.

• Chop herbs just before using so the flavors will be pungent and fresh.

• Plant a bay tree in your garden or in a pot—they are very hardy and nothing beats the flavor of a freshly picked bay leaf.

• Check your pantry—be ruthless and discard anything past its expiration date. Spices lose their flavor over time, so buy little and often. Dried beans, peas, and lentils—believe it or not—also lose their quality if kept too long. So use or lose!

BAKING CAKES AND PASTRIES

• Weigh and measure all the ingredients before you start. In baking, accuracy in measurement, oven heat, and timing is the key to success. Always follow the recipe exactly.

• Leave plenty of time to preheat the oven before baking—at least 30 minutes is a good guide. (You can buy special oven thermometers to check that your oven temperature is accurate.)

• Don't try to make pie crusts in the middle of a hot day—at least do it in the early morning or late evening. The cooler your kitchen and your hands, the better the crust will be.

• Always chill the butter when making dough. Chill the dough for about 30 minutes before rolling, then chill the uncooked pie crust before baking. The dough heats up as you work on it—chilling lets it cool and rest so it won't shrink so much in the oven.

OILS

• Olive oil is not only the King of Oils, it is also a good all-round oil for all methods of cooking except Asian or Indian.

• For Indian and Asian cooking, I use safflower oil, peanut oil, or other good-quality non-olive oil.

• I avoid using oils labeled simply "vegetable oil"—they are often extracted by heat treatment, a method that can destroy many of the good nutrients in oil.

• Always have a spout on the top of your bottle of oil—it limits the amount that pours out and gives you accurate direction when drizzling over dishes before serving.

KNIVES

• Have at least two good knives and sharpen them frequently.

• I use a whetstone rather than a steel to get a good sharp edge.

DRINKS

• Better to buy too much than too little—you can always use the extra at your next party.

• Bubbly Allow ½–¾ bottle per person (6 glasses in a bottle, or 8 if making cocktails).

• Wine Allow 1 bottle per person. In summer, allow 3 bottles of white to 1 of red.

• Liquor, cocktails, and Liquor-based punches There are 16 measures in a fifth of liquor. Allow 3 per person during a 2-hour party.

• Sparkling water/soft drinks Don't forget the non-drinkers, "designated drivers," and kids. Have lots and keep it cold!

everyday entertaining

Friends often quote complicated menus and ask me if cookbook authors are connected to the real world. Well, I am, and I want to help you to cook good food at home—food you will enjoy creating and everyone will love eating. For everyday entertaining, it is more important than ever to keep the menu simple and to be as prepared as possible.

The recipes in this section are designed to fit in with busy lives, and perfect for informal, quick, or impromptu entertaining. Turn, for example, to Effortless Entertaining (page 40), Dinner in Advance (page 60), or Market Picnic (page 14), which I have devised to help minimize your time in the kitchen, while still giving stunning and delicious results.

My advice to you is to keep a well-stocked pantry. You don't want to be shopping for all the ingredients on a busy weekday, so if you have a few useful backup supplies on hand, it only leaves the fresh ingredients to find on the day. Then just pick a menu, adapt and adjust it to suit your tastes or mood, and start cooking.

market picnic

MENU
SUGGESTIONS

Parma Ham

Salami

Potato and
Tarragon Cake

Mixed Washed
Leaves

Pâté en Croûte

Sliced Ham
and Parsley
Mousse

Pissaladière

Bread

Goat Cheese

Peaches

Chocolate
Opera Cake

Apple Custard
Tart

Hazelnut
Cookies

Vanilla Yogurts

TO DRINK

Hard Cider

market shopping

Treat yourself and take time out to
visit your local farmers' market, where
the producers sell their own goods, so
you can chat about the quality and
taste. It's such a treat, as well as being
a very sensual experience, to shop for
food in a market. It often looks so raw
and real, with the stallholders full of
stories and love for their produce.
Don't be afraid to ask questions—in
my experience, they have a wealth of
information that they are only too
happy to share with their customers.

This menu is just to give you an idea
of what you can buy to create an
instant no-cook picnic. Delicacies will
vary from place to place, but it's
always fun to be adventurous and try
something that you're not familiar with,
be it a cheese, pâté, tart, or simply an
unusual bread.

THE WORK PLAN

on the day

- When you go to a market, always take plenty of small change. (I think it's rude to hand over a large note for a small bag of produce.)
- Have a large box or basket in which to carry your fresh purchases or, better still, take a strong friend to help gather and carry.
- What could be simpler: shop, travel to your chosen destination, spread out the rug, pour a drink, and let everyone unwrap your treasures and enjoy your easy, inspirational, open air picnic.

the scene

After gathering your market purchases together in baskets, boxes, and bags, find a quiet, shady spot under a tree, spread out a cloth, and set out all the delicious produce for everyone to unwrap.

the style

This is really made by the surroundings and the goods you buy. Some producers take such pride in their packaging and presentation—beautiful sheets of waxed paper to wrap meats and cheeses, pretty boxes to protect tarts and cakes, crisp paper bags for bread, and pretty baskets for fruit. All you need is a beautiful picnic blanket or cloth on which to set out your feast, plus flatware and glasses.

mediterranean lunch

THE MENU

FOR 8 PEOPLE

Char-Grilled Jumbo Shrimp with Citrus Wedges

Summer Vegetable Salad

White Bean and Tomato Salad

Baby Leaf Salad

Spring Garlic Dressing

Crusty Bread

Strawberry Tart

TO DRINK

Rosé

the scene

Just think of eating outside in the sunshine and cooking shrimp on an outdoor grill. Add some char-grilled vegetables bathed in extra virgin olive oil and a mixed summer leaf salad with fresh garlic dressing, then mop up all the juices with bread from a local bakery. All you need is a sunny day and this menu can be created in your own garden. The meal is very informal and perfect to serve at large, friendly gatherings. Your guests can help you create this feast. Put plates, napkins, knives, and forks onto a tray and ask friends to set the table. Someone can help with the grill and others can make the salads.

the style

Decorate the table with simple flowers from the garden, wild grasses gathered from a meadow, or bowls of ripe summer fruit, piled high. Provide a few little bowls with water and sliced lemons to dip and wash fingers, plus lots of napkins for laps and chins. Have everything you need set out on the table, so you don't have to keep getting up (and missing out on the laughter), then just graze your way through a sunny afternoon.

summer vegetable salad

6 baby artichokes, stems removed

2 lb. asparagus, ends trimmed

1/2 cup olive oil

2 large red bell peppers, quartered and seeded

5 zucchini, sliced lengthwise

freshly squeezed juice of 1 lemon

sea salt and freshly ground black pepper

serves 8

Bring a large saucepan of water to a boil. Add the artichokes and simmer for 30–40 minutes, or until tender.

Meanwhile, put the asparagus into a plastic bag with 3 tablespoons of the olive oil and shake well. Heat a stove-top grill pan until hot, add the asparagus, and cook for 5 minutes, turning frequently, until lightly charred. Remove and set aside.

Add the bell pepper pieces to the pan, skin side down, and cook for about 7 minutes, or until the skin is charred and blistered. Transfer to a small bowl, cover with a lid, and let cool.

Add the zucchini to the pan and cook for 4 minutes on each side, until lightly charred.

Drain the artichokes and halve them lengthwise. If they are small enough, they should have no "choke," but scrape out the area with a teaspoon to make sure. Remove and discard the skins from the peppers and cut the flesh into strips.

Arrange all the vegetables in a large bowl, sprinkle with salt, pepper, the remaining olive oil, and lemon juice, then serve.

char-grilled jumbo shrimp with citrus wedges

For extra flavor and aroma, always grill shrimp with their shells on. Toss them in olive oil before adding to the grill and cook just until the flesh is just opaque—don't overcook or they will be dry and tasteless. Buy as many shrimp as you can afford—there will never be any left over.

4 lb. jumbo shrimp, shell on

about 1/3 cup olive oil

4 lemons or 6 limes, cut into wedges, to serve

serves 8

Put the shrimp into a large bowl or plastic bag, add the olive oil, and shake to coat. Cook on a preheated grill until the shells are red and the flesh is opaque, then serve on a large platter with lemon or lime wedges for squeezing.

white bean and tomato salad

1½ lb. new potatoes, unpeeled

2 cans cannellini beans, 15 oz. each, drained and rinsed, about 4 cups

1 lb. ripe tomatoes, quartered

4 scallions, sliced

a bunch of flat-leaf parsley, chopped

¼ cup extra virgin olive oil

freshly squeezed juice of 1 lemon

sea salt and freshly ground black pepper

serves 8

Cook the potatoes in a large saucepan of boiling, salted water for about 20 minutes, or until tender when pierced with a knife. Drain. When cool enough to handle, cut into wedges and put into a large bowl.

Add the beans, tomatoes, scallions, and parsley. Sprinkle with olive oil, lemon juice, salt, and pepper. Toss gently and serve.

baby leaf salad

Baby leaves (mesclun) with their contrasting flavors—sweet, crisp, bitter—are widely available in farmers' markets and supermarkets. When you wash salad leaves, always dry them in a salad spinner, as there's nothing worse than a soggy salad.

1 lb. small mixed salad leaves, washed and dried

spring garlic dressing (right)

serves 8

Check that all the leaves are clean. Trim off any dead ends and discard any droopy leaves. Put the leaves into a large bowl and serve the dressing separately.

spring garlic dressing

If you are lucky enough to find spring garlic, use it to make this surprisingly mild salad dressing. Spring garlic bulbs are larger than usual and the most beautiful pink. This dressing doesn't need any mixing or shaking—serve it with a little spoon so guests can help themselves. It tastes great and looks like a work of art.

1 large garlic bulb, spring garlic if possible, finely sliced

½ cup olive oil

2 tablespoons balsamic vinegar

sea salt and freshly ground black pepper

serves 8

Put the garlic into a small serving bowl. Add the oil and balsamic vinegar, with salt and pepper to taste, then serve.

THE WORK PLAN

the day before

- Make the pie crust. Store in an airtight container.

on the day

- Cook the artichokes. Drain and let cool. Cook the remaining vegetables for the summer vegetable salad in the grill pan and assemble.
- Assemble the strawberry tart.
- Light the grill.
- Cook the potatoes.
- Make the bean and tomato salad.

just before serving

- Make the spring garlic dressing.
- Cook the shrimp on the preheated grill.

strawberry tart

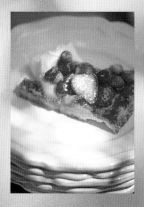

When any fruit is abundant and in season, I feel it just has to be used in a tart with sweet and crumbling crust. This mixture of wild and regular strawberries is just delicious—the tiny wild strawberries look so beautiful and are packed with flavor. If you can't find them, use the same weight in regular. Any other soft fruit can be used, just make sure you pile the tart high with fruit.

Put the flour into a mixing bowl and add the butter. Using your fingertips, rub the butter into the flour until it looks like bread crumbs. Add the sugar and mix. Make a well in the middle and add 2 of the egg yolks. Mix with a round-bladed knife, using cutting motions, until the mixture forms a ball, adding an extra egg yolk if needed. Dust your hands lightly with flour, bring the mixture together, and transfer to a lightly floured, cool surface.

Roll out the dough to just larger than the pan. Line the pan with the dough, prick all over with a fork, and chill for 20 minutes. Cook in a preheated oven at 350°F for 20 minutes, then reduce to 300°F and cook for a further 20 minutes. Remove from the oven and let cool, then transfer to a flat serving plate and cover with plastic wrap until needed.

Put the strawberry jelly into a small saucepan and heat gently until thin and smooth. Remove and set aside to cool a little while you pile the strawberries into the cooked pie crust, cutting any very large berries into smaller pieces. Spoon the strawberry jelly over the strawberries and serve with cream or plain yogurt mixed with honey.

2 cups all-purpose flour

2 sticks butter, cut into small pieces

¾ cup brown sugar

2–3 egg yolks, beaten

¾ cup strawberry jelly, about 7 oz.

8 oz. wild strawberries

1½ lb. regular strawberries, hulls removed

heavy cream or plain yogurt mixed with honey, to serve

a nonstick tart pan, 12 inches diameter

serves 8

fall dinner

THE MENU

FOR 6 PEOPLE

Tuscan Bean and Spicy
Sausage Soup

Focaccia

Roasted Pheasant
Breasts with Bacon,
Shallots, and
Mushrooms

Marbled Chocolate
Risotto

or

Fruit Crumbles

TO DRINK
Merlot, Sangiovese

the scene

When the days start to draw in and
the leaves fall from the trees, I must
admit I get a little sad, so I cheer
myself up by indulging in the fabulous
seasonal foods available at this time
of year. It's a great way to banish the
cold weather blues.

the style

Move the table to the cosiest part of
your home and create a snug feeling
for enjoying the seasonal bounty.
If you are lucky enough to have a
fireplace, pull up a table and comfy
armchairs in front of a roaring fire.

tuscan bean and spicy sausage soup

If you want to use dried, rather than canned, cannellini beans, measure 1 1/4 cups, soak them overnight, drain, and put into a saucepan with water to cover. Bring to a boil and simmer for 10 minutes, then drain. Return to the pan, again with cold water to cover. Bring to a boil and simmer for 1 hour, removing any foam that rises to the surface. Stir occasionally.

2 tablespoons olive oil

2 red onions, chopped

2 garlic cloves, chopped

4 oz. pancetta or prosciutto, chopped

1 carrot, chopped

2 celery stalks, chopped

1 can cannellini beans, 15 oz., drained, about 2 cups

3 spicy Italian sausages

1 quart chicken stock

1 bay leaf

a bunch of flat-leaf parsley, chopped

sea salt and freshly ground black pepper

serves 6

Put the oil into a saucepan, heat well, then add the onion, garlic, pancetta, carrot, and celery and cook over low heat for 10 minutes until softened but not browned. Add the beans, sausages, stock, bay leaf, salt, and pepper. Bring to a boil, cover with a lid, and simmer for 30 minutes. Skim off any excess fat, then remove the sausages and slice them diagonally. Return the sausages to the soup and add the parsley. Serve in large, heated soup plates.

focaccia

3 cups bread flour, plus extra for dusting

1 package (1/4 oz.) active dry yeast

1/2 cup extra virgin olive oil, plus extra for greasing and brushing

12 cherry tomatoes

leaves from a sprig of rosemary

coarse sea salt

a baking tray, lightly greased with olive oil

serves 6

Put the flour and yeast into a food processor. With the motor on low speed, gradually add the oil and 1 1/4 cups warm water until the mixture forms a soft dough. Remove to a lightly floured surface and knead for 5 minutes. Transfer to the prepared baking tray and, using your hands, spread it evenly to the edges. Brush all over with oil, push the cherry tomatoes and rosemary leaves lightly into the surface of the dough at regular intervals and sprinkle sea salt over the top. Cover with a damp, clean dish cloth and put in a warm place for 40 minutes until doubled in size.

Bake in a preheated oven at 400°F for 20 minutes, until golden.

the day before

- Make and cook the fruit crumbles.
- Make the soup, but don't slice the sausages or add the parsley.

on the day

- Make the focaccia.
- Wrap the pheasant breasts with bacon, prepare the shallots and mushrooms, cover, and chill until 1 hour before cooking.
- Prepare the risotto ingredients, but don't cook until just before serving.

just before serving

- Reheat the soup, adding the sliced sausages and parsley.
- Cook the pheasant.
- Cook the risotto.
- Heat the fruit crumbles in a preheated oven at 300°F for 20 minutes.

roasted pheasant breasts with bacon, shallots, and mushrooms

Depending on size, you may need two breasts per person—this is something you can decide when shopping, The look-and-choose, visual method is always best. If you are offered a choice between hen and cock pheasant, buy the hen—they have better breast meat and are plumper. Cooking a whole pheasant is more economical and will serve 2–3 people, but involves all that last-minute carving and it never looks as good. If pheasant is hard to find, use guinea fowl.

6 plump pheasant breasts

12 slices bacon

6 sprigs of thyme

3 fresh bay leaves, halved

2 tablespoons butter

1 tablespoon olive oil

12 small shallots

½ cup dry sherry

6 portobello mushrooms, quartered

6 thick slices French bread

8 oz. watercress

sea salt and freshly cracked black pepper

serves 6

Remove the skin from the pheasant breasts and discard it. Wrap 2 slices of bacon around each breast, inserting a sprig of thyme and half a bay leaf between the pheasant and the bacon.

Put the butter and oil into a large roasting pan and set on top of the stove over high heat. Add the pheasant breasts, shallots, sherry, mushrooms, salt, and pepper. Turn the pheasant breasts in the mixture until they are well coated. Cook on the upper rack of a preheated oven at 375°F for 25 minutes. Remove from the oven and let rest for 5 minutes. Put the bread onto plates, then add the watercress, mushrooms, shallots, and pheasant. Spoon over any cooking juices and serve.

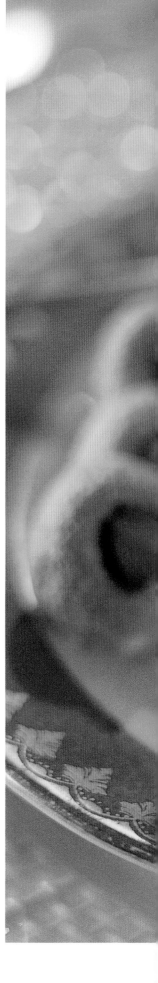

Trust me: this chocolate risotto is the best. Soft grains of rice gently cooked in milk, swathed in melted chocolate— don't say you aren't tempted!

marbled chocolate risotto

This dish is so wicked—it's my 21st century version of rice pudding. For a real treat, soak the golden raisins in brandy or whiskey for 2 hours first.

2³/₄ cups milk

2 tablespoons sugar

4 tablespoons butter

²/₃ cup risotto rice, such as arborio or carnaroli

¹/₃ cup hazelnuts, chopped, about 2 oz.

¹/₃ cup golden raisins

2 squares (2 oz.) milk chocolate, grated

2 squares (2 oz.) bittersweet chocolate, grated

serves 6

Put the milk and sugar into a saucepan and heat until just simmering. Melt the butter in a large, heavy-bottom saucepan, add the rice, and stir well to coat the grains. Add a ladle of the warm milk and mix well. When the milk has been absorbed, add more and continue, stirring frequently, until it has all been added and the rice is soft. This will take about 12–15 minutes. Add the hazelnuts and golden raisins and mix well. Remove from the heat and add the grated chocolate, stirring briefly to create a marbled effect. Serve at once.

fruit crumbles

My favorite crumbles are always made with red berries, because they are so juicy and delicious. However, I always include a baking apple to add a little texture.

1 cup all-purpose flour

6 tablespoons butter, cut into small pieces

1/2 cup firmly packed brown sugar

2/3 cup rolled oats

1 lb. mixed berries and fruit, such as blackberries, red currants, black currants, raspberries, strawberries, or plums, pitted if necessary, about 3 cups

1 large baking apple, cored, peeled, and sliced

1/4 cup sugar

cream or real custard (page 53), to serve

6 ramekins

serves 6

To make the crumble topping, put the flour into a bowl and rub in the butter with your fingertips until it disappears into the flour. Add the brown sugar and oats and mix well.

Remove and discard any stalks from the berries and fruits. Cut into even pieces, if necessary, and put into a bowl. Stir in the apple. Divide the fruit between the ramekins, then sprinkle with sugar and the crumble topping. Cook in a preheated oven at 350°F for about 40 minutes until the top is golden and bubbling. Serve with cream or real custard.

the scene

For a midweek after-work supper, this menu is very flexible, with an easy salad, the risotto, then the option of baked apples or toasted oat yogurts, according to taste and what's in the pantry. It's all quick to prepare, to fit in with a busy working day.

the style

Sit around a simply clad table, put the food in the middle, and dig in. Serve the risotto straight from the pan.

express dining

THE MENU

SERVES 4

Poached Egg and Anchovy Salad

Classic Risotto

Toasted Oat Yogurt and Crushed Red Berries

or

Baked Stuffed Apples with Butterscotch

TO DRINK

Pinot Grigio, crisp Riesling, Sangiovese, Merlot

poached egg and anchovy salad

Using a stick blender is a quick and easy way to get a good, emulsified dressing. I always make double the amount because this dressing is so good.

Put the mixed leaves into a large bowl and add the capers. Put the anchovies into a small bowl and add the mustard powder, vinegar, and oil. Blend with a stick blender until emulsified.

Fill a large, shallow saucepan with hot water, heat to a gentle simmer, and crack each egg into a separate cup. Stir the water in one direction to create a whirlpool. Gently slip each egg into the water and return to a gentle simmer. Cover, remove the pan from the heat, and let stand for 6 minutes for softly poached eggs.

Meanwhile, reserve a few of the chives and add the remainder to the salad. Sprinkle with salt and pepper. Reserve a little dressing for serving and pour the remainder over the salad. Toss well and put onto serving plates. Remove the eggs from the water using a slotted spoon and dry underneath the spoon with paper towels to absorb excess water. Put an egg on top of each salad. Spoon over a little dressing, top with a few chives, and serve.

8 oz. mixed salad leaves, washed and dried

1 tablespoon capers, drained and rinsed

4 anchovy fillets in oil, drained and finely chopped

1 teaspoon English mustard powder

1 tablespoon white wine vinegar

3 tablespoons extra virgin olive oil

4 eggs

sea salt and freshly ground black pepper

a bunch of chives, chopped, to serve

serves 4

THE WORK PLAN

the day before

- Make the butterscotch sauce, cover, and chill. (Reheat in a saucepan.)

on the day

- Prepare and stuff the apples, cover, and set aside.
- Make the toasted oat yogurts, cover, and chill.

just before serving

- Make the salad dressing, cook the eggs, and assemble the salad.
- Bake the apples.
- Prepare and cook the risotto.

classic risotto

If you are a keen cook you may make all your own stock, which is brilliant and I admire you, but I only do it sometimes! Luckily, it's possible to buy good stock.

1 quart chicken or vegetable stock	¹/₂ teaspoon saffron threads
6 tablespoons butter	²/₃ cup dry vermouth
1 tablespoon olive oil	4 oz. freshly grated Parmesan cheese, 1¹/₄ cups, plus extra to serve
4 shallots, finely chopped	
2 cups risotto rice, such as arborio or carnaroli	sea salt and freshly ground black pepper

serves 4

Put the stock into a saucepan and heat until simmering. Put 4 tablespoons of the butter into a large saucepan, add the oil, and heat until the butter has melted. Add the shallots and sauté for 5 minutes, until softened but not browned.

Add the rice and stir until coated. Add the saffron and just enough hot stock to cover the rice. Simmer gently, stirring frequently, and adding more stock as it is absorbed by the rice.

When all the stock has been added and almost absorbed, about 12–15 minutes, add the vermouth, Parmesan, and remaining butter. Add salt and pepper to taste and simmer until the rice is soft and the sauce rich and creamy. Sprinkle with Parmesan and serve.

toasted oat yogurt and crushed red berries

Baking the oats adds a caramel crunch to this simple dessert. If you don't have the berries, use whatever fruit you have already—bananas, apples, pears, peaches, or nectarines are all good.

²/₃ **cup rolled oats**

1¹/₂ **tablespoons brown sugar**

10 oz. mixed berries, about 2 cups

1 cup plain yogurt

¹/₄ **cup honey**

a baking tray, lined with parchment paper

serves 4

Put the rolled oats and sugar into a bowl and mix. Sprinkle evenly over the baking tray and put under a preheated broiler. Toast until golden and caramelized, then remove and let cool on the sheet.

Put half the berries into a bowl and coarsely crush with the back of a spoon. Add the yogurt and toasted oats and mix lightly until marbled. Spoon into glasses and top with the remaining berries and honey. Chill until ready to serve.

I can never choose between the toasted oat yogurts and baked stuffed apples—they are both so perfect and simple. If you are like me, make both.

4 tablespoons butter

3 tablespoons brown sugar

1/3 cup raisins

2/3 cup dried cranberries

2/3 cup dried cherries

6 baking apples, cored

1 cinnamon stick, broken lengthwise into 6 strips

BUTTERSCOTCH

4 tablespoons butter

2/3 cup brown sugar

2/3 cup light corn syrup

1/2 cup heavy cream

an ovenproof dish, big enough to fit the apples, lightly buttered

serves 4

baked stuffed apples with butterscotch

Butterscotch is absolutely wicked stuff, but occasionally a wicked must. It can be made 2 weeks in advance and stored in a screwtop jar in the refrigerator. Try it hot or cold with ice cream, bananas, or chocolate cake—it's always a winner for people with a sweet tooth. I always make 2 extra apples, for seconds.

Put the butter and sugar into a bowl, beat until creamy, then stir in the dried fruits. Using a small, sharp knife, score the skin all the way around the middle of each apple, to prevent them bursting. Put the apples into the prepared dish, stuff with the dried fruit mixture, and put a piece of cinnamon into each. Bake on the middle shelf of a preheated oven at 375°F for 20 minutes, then reduce to 300°F and bake for a further 25 minutes, until soft and bubbling.

To make the butterscotch, put the butter, sugar, and syrup into a saucepan. Heat slowly over low heat until melted, then simmer gently for 5 minutes. Remove from the heat and gradually add the cream, stirring constantly, until it has all been added and the sauce is smooth. Serve spooned over the baked apples.

the scene

Move tables and chairs out into the garden—standing and having to balance plates and glasses can spoil a delicious meal. Otherwise, you can put large tablecloths or blankets on the ground and provide big soft pillows.

the style

When the sun comes out and the garden is full of flowers, those outdoor grills emerge from everybody's garden sheds or garages. Grills come in all shapes and sizes and, although the gas ones are convenient and easy, I do think that, for real grill flavor, you need coals or wood. The menu is mixed tapas-style, with food to suit all tastes.

THE WORK PLAN

the day before

- Make the dough for the tarts and store in the refrigerator.
- Marinate the lamb overnight.
- Slow-roast the tomatoes for the salsa, cover, and chill.

on the day

- Assemble and cook the fruit tarts.
- Make the bean salad, cover, and store at room temperature.
- Cook the croutons and lardons for the frisée salad.
- Preheat the outdoor grill. This will take at least an hour.

just before serving

- Grill the lamb and put the chicken wings into the oven to roast.
- Make the salsa for the swordfish and prepare the eggplant for the grill.
- Grill the eggplant and zucchini.
- Make the couscous salad.
- Assemble the eggplant and feta salad and the frisée salad.
- Grill the swordfish.
- Add the sticky sauce to the chicken.

relaxed garden barbecue

swordfish with salsa

Swordfish is brought to life with this delicious half-cooked salsa. Slow-roasting softens the tomatoes and intensifies their flavor. This salsa is a much-loved recipe that I serve with many different fish and meat dishes. It's also great served on a bowl of fresh pasta such as ravioli.

1 lb. cherry tomatoes

2 red onions, finely chopped

1/2 teaspoon hot red pepper flakes

a large bunch of flat-leaf parsley, chopped

1/3 cup olive oil

freshly squeezed juice of 2 limes

8 swordfish steaks, 4 oz. each

sea salt and freshly ground black pepper

serves 8

To make the salsa, put the tomatoes into a roasting pan and cook in a preheated oven at 300°F for 1 hour. Remove and let cool.

Transfer to a bowl, add the onions, pepper flakes, parsley, oil, lime juice, salt, and pepper. Mix well.

Sprinkle the swordfish steaks with salt and pepper. Cook over medium heat on a preheated grill for 4–6 minutes on each side, depending on thickness, until just cooked through. Serve with the salsa.

honeyed chicken wings

These really should be called Last Lick Chicken Wings—anyone who eats them removes every morsel of flavor and sticky meat from the bones. Just watch out that they don't burn in the oven.

16 chicken wings

1 cup honey

1 cup chile sauce

sea salt and freshly ground black pepper

a bunch of radishes, trimmed, to serve (optional)

serves 8

Put the chicken wings into an oiled roasting pan and cook in a preheated oven at 400°F for 40 minutes, turning them after 20 minutes so they brown evenly.

Meanwhile, put the honey and sweet chile sauce into a small saucepan. Add salt and pepper to taste and bring to a boil. Pour the sauce over the chicken, mix well, and let cool. Serve with radishes, if using.

grilled zucchini

8 zucchini, cut lengthwise into 1/2-inch slices

olive oil

balsamic vinegar

sea salt and freshly ground black pepper

serves 8

Cook the zucchini slices over medium heat on a preheated grill for 3–4 minutes on each side, until lightly charred. Remove to a plate and sprinkle with oil, vinegar, salt, and pepper. Serve hot, warm, or cold.

turmeric lamb with couscous salad

I use lamb fillets for this dish—my butcher cuts the fillet from the cut which forms the crown roast. You can use any tender boneless roasting cut of lamb, but the cooking time will vary according to thickness. If you use a leg, have it boned and butterflied to lie flat on the grill.

TURMERIC LAMB

3 teaspoons ground turmeric

1 teaspoon ground cinnamon

3 teaspoons medium curry powder

2 garlic cloves, chopped

3 tablespoons olive oil

1/4 cup honey

3 lb. boneless lamb, such as boned and butterflied leg

sea salt and freshly ground black pepper

COUSCOUS SALAD

13 oz. couscous, about 2 cups

1/2 teaspoon saffron threads

2 tablespoons butter

2 tablespoons olive oil

4 onions, sliced

1 garlic clove, chopped

2/3 cup shelled pistachios, coarsely chopped

grated zest and freshly squeezed juice of 2 unwaxed lemons

a large bunch of cilantro, chopped

sea salt and freshly ground black pepper

serves 8

Put the turmeric, cinnamon, curry powder, garlic, oil, and honey into a bowl, add salt and pepper to taste, and stir well. Trim any excess fat off the lamb and rub the spice mixture all over. Transfer to a dish, cover, and chill overnight.

To make the couscous salad, put the couscous and saffron into a large bowl. Pour over 1 3/4 cups boiling water, mix, and set aside, covered, for 15 minutes until all the liquid has been absorbed.

Meanwhile, heat the butter and oil in a large skillet, add the onions, and cook for 8 minutes until golden and slightly frizzled. Add the garlic and cook for a further 2 minutes, then add the onions and garlic to the prepared couscous.

Add the pistachio nuts, lemon zest and juice, cilantro, salt, and pepper, mix well, and set aside.

Cook the lamb on a hot preheated grill for about 25 minutes for medium rare, turning them frequently and basting with any extra marinade. Remove to a board, slice, and serve with the couscous salad.

classic frisée and bacon salad

2 heads of frisée, leaves separated

2 shallots, finely chopped

2 tablespoons olive oil, plus extra to serve

1 lb. thick-cut bacon, chopped

2 tablespoons red wine vinegar

a bunch of basil, leaves torn

sea salt and freshly ground black pepper

serves 8

Put the frisée into a large serving bowl and add the shallots.

Heat the olive oil in a large skillet, add the bacon, and cook until brown and crispy. If serving immediately, add to the lettuce and shallots. Otherwise, remove to a plate and let cool.

Just before serving, add the bacon, olive oil, vinegar, basil, salt, and pepper to the bowl. Toss well and serve.

white and green bean salad

The ingredients for this salad are very flexible: cannellini beans or chickpeas could be used in place of the lima beans, and other green beans or peas—such as snowpeas, sugar snaps, or sliced runner beans—in place of the regular green beans.

3 tablespoons olive oil

1 tablespoon balsamic vinegar

2 cans lima beans, 15 oz. each, drained and rinsed, about 4 cups

10 oz. green beans, trimmed

2 oz. pumpkin seeds, about 1/2 cup

sea salt and freshly ground black pepper

serves 8

Put the oil and vinegar into a large serving bowl. Stir in the lima beans and set aside. Cook the green beans in a saucepan of boiling, salted water for 3 minutes. Drain, refresh in several changes of cold water until cool, then drain again. Add the green beans and pumpkin seeds to the bowl and stir. Sprinkle with salt and pepper and serve.

baked seasonal fruit tarts with pouring cream

Once the rich, simple dough has been made, these delicious tarts are very easy. You just fill with seasonal fruit and bake them slowly. Choose from apricots, plums, cherries, apples, blueberries, peaches, and nectarines. Don't worry if the dough breaks as you line the pans—just patch any holes or cracks with the trimmings. It will be topped with lovely fruit, so no one will know!

4 cups all-purpose flour, plus extra for dusting

5½ sticks softened butter, cut into pieces

1¾ cups confectioners' sugar, plus extra for dusting

3 egg yolks

3 lb. fruit, pitted if necessary

2 cups light cream, to serve

2 loose-bottom tart pans, 10 inches diameter

serves 8

To make the dough, put the flour, butter, and confectioners' sugar into a food processor and blend briefly. Add the egg yolks and blend until the mixture forms a ball. Divide in half, wrap both pieces in plastic wrap, and chill for 40 minutes.

Put one piece of dough onto a cool, lightly floured surface and gently knead to a flat disk. Roll out into a shape large enough to fit the tart pan, dusting lightly with flour to stop the dough sticking to the surface. Roll the dough around a floured rolling pin and unroll over the tart pan. Gently press the dough into the pan, pressing out any air pockets, then roll the pin over the top of the pan to remove any excess dough. Repeat with the remaining dough and tart pan, cover, and chill for 25 minutes.

Prepare the fruit and slice, halve, or leave whole, depending on size. Arrange in the chilled, unbaked pie crusts. Working from the outside in, pack in all the fruit (it will shrink while cooking). Cook in a preheated oven at 350°F for 35 minutes, then reduce to 300°F and cook for a further 55 minutes until the crust is golden and crisp. Remove and dust generously with confectioners' sugar. Serve hot, warm, or cold with pouring cream.

eggplant and feta salad

If you have a specialist Greek or Middle Eastern food shop near you, buy feta cheese there: they will have a good range of varying sharpness and texture. Taste and choose the one for you.

½ cup olive oil

1 teaspoon ground cumin

1 teaspoon ground coriander

3 medium eggplant, cut into 1-inch slices

8 oz. feta cheese, crumbled

1 cup pine nuts, toasted in a dry skillet

a bunch of mint, chopped

sea salt and freshly ground black pepper

serves 8

Put the oil, cumin, and coriander into a bowl, then stir in salt and pepper to taste. Brush both sides of the eggplant slices with the spiced oil and cook on a hot preheated grill for 3–4 minutes on each side, until soft and lightly charred.

Transfer to a large bowl, then stir in the feta, pine nuts, and mint. Serve warm, at room temperature, or cold.

effortless entertaining

the scene

Visual appeal is important to this cook, but the cooking has to be effortless too. The menu is simple and easy to prepare, and looks oh-so-perfect in this stylish setting.

the style

Beautiful and slightly serene, this is for the cook who would rather concentrate, not on elaborate cooking, but on the table—all the latest looks for china and flatware. The food sits beautifully in this amazing setting—one for the style guru!

THE WORK PLAN

the day before

- Make and cook the apple bake, or roast the peaches and stew the rhubarb.
- Prepare the cream, cover, and chill.

on the day

- Roast the eggplant and tomatoes and make the dressing.
- Peel and chop the tomatoes to go with the guinea fowl or chicken.

just before serving

- Trim and cook the artichokes.
- Assemble the salad and broil the prosciutto.
- Cook the spaghetti and guinea fowl or chicken.
- Assemble the peaches and rhubarb.

THE MENU

FOR 4 PEOPLE

Easy Artichokes

Roasted Eggplant and Prosciutto Salad

Guinea Fowl and Asparagus Spaghetti

Norwegian Apple Bake

or

Roasted Peaches with Rhubarb and Mascarpone Cream

TO DRINK

Chardonnay, Zinfandel

easy artichokes

Put out extra napkins—eating artichokes is a hands-on experience!

4 medium artichokes, stems removed

extra virgin olive oil, to serve

serves 4

Put the artichokes into a large saucepan, stem side down, cover with water, and bring to a boil. Simmer for 40 minutes, until an outer leaf pulls away easily. Drain well and turn the artichokes upside down in a colander to cool and drain off excess water. Serve warm, with olive oil for dipping.

roasted eggplant and prosciutto salad

Prosciutto makes wonderful crispy bacon, so start cooking and impress with your relaxed and easy new-found kitchen skills.

8 oz. cherry tomatoes, about 1½ cups

2 small eggplant, sliced lengthwise

2 tablespoons olive oil

4 slices prosciutto

a bunch of arugula

sea salt and freshly ground black pepper

DRESSING

1 tablespoon balsamic vinegar

1 tablespoon Dijon mustard

3 tablespoons extra virgin olive oil

sea salt and freshly ground black pepper

serves 4

Slice off and discard the top of each tomato, then put them, cut side up, into an oiled roasting pan. Add the eggplant. Sprinkle with the olive oil, salt, and pepper. Cook in a preheated oven at 350°F for 15 minutes, then reduce to 300°F for a further 15 minutes, until the tomatoes have burst their skins. Remove from the oven and set aside. Cook the prosciutto under a hot, preheated broiler for about 3 minutes on each side, until crisp.

To make the dressing, put the vinegar and mustard into a small bowl and mix until smooth. Gradually add the oil, mixing well, then add salt and pepper to taste. Arrange the arugula and roasted eggplant and tomatoes on plates and spoon over the dressing. Top with the prosciutto and serve warm or at room temperature.

2 large tomatoes

10 oz. dried spaghetti

4 guinea fowl breasts, or
chicken breasts, 4 oz. each

10 oz. asparagus, trimmed

8 oz. fine green beans

1/4 cup olive oil, plus extra
to serve

3 oz. black olives, such
as niçoise or kalamata,
pitted and chopped,
about 1/2 cup

sea salt and freshly ground
black pepper

fresh shavings of
Parmesan cheese, to serve

serves 4

guinea fowl and asparagus spaghetti

This is my one-pot-wonder, and I just love the combination of clean and fresh flavors.
The spaghetti absorbs the rich stock, so tastes good and looks fantastic. Try this method
using any other boneless cuts of meat or fish that need very quick cooking.

Cut a cross in the top of each tomato, put into
a bowl, and cover with boiling water. Drain after
30 seconds, then peel and chop.

Bring a large saucepan of water to a boil and add
the spaghetti. Stir, then put the guinea fowl breasts
on top of the spaghetti. Cover with a lid and
simmer for 8 minutes, then add the asparagus
and beans. Replace the lid and cook for a further
3 minutes, until the spaghetti and guinea fowl
are cooked. Drain, reserving the cooking liquid
for a soup or sauce.

Transfer the guinea fowl to a carving board and
cover loosely with foil. Return the spaghetti to the
saucepan over medium heat and add the oil, olives,
tomatoes, salt, and pepper. Cook, stirring constantly,
for 2 minutes, then transfer to warmed serving
plates. Slice the guinea fowl and arrange on top
of the spaghetti. Top with Parmesan shavings,
drizzle with olive oil, sprinkle with salt and pepper,
then serve.

roasted peaches with rhubarb and mascarpone cream

Roasted peaches have been around a long time, but I have added an extra twist with the stewed rhubarb and cream.

4 soft, juicy peaches or nectarines, halved crosswise and pitted

10 oz. rhubarb, chopped into 1-inch chunks

1/4 cup heavy cream

1/3 cup sugar

1/4 cup mascarpone cheese

a baking dish, lightly buttered

serves 4

Put the peach halves into the buttered baking dish, skin side down, and roast at the top of a preheated oven at 400°F for 15 minutes until caramelized and softened.

Meanwhile, put the rhubarb into a small saucepan, add 1 tablespoon water, and heat until bubbling. Reduce the heat to low, cover with a lid, and cook for 10 minutes. Remove from the heat and set aside to cool, with the lid on.

Put the cream into a bowl and whip lightly. Add the sugar and mascarpone and mix until smooth. Add the stewed rhubarb and stir briefly, adding more sugar if needed. Serve with the roasted peaches, with any juices spooned over the top.

norwegian apple bake

This is such a good standby dessert—usually, you will have all the dry ingredients in your pantry. You can use any kind of apples, pears, or even plums.

2 eggs

1 1/4 cups sugar

1 stick butter

2/3 cup milk

4 baking apples, cored, peeled, and sliced

1 cup plus 2 tablespoons self-rising flour

1/2 teaspoon freshly grated nutmeg

heavy cream or vanilla ice cream, to serve

a shallow ovenproof dish, 12 inches diameter, buttered

serves 4

Put the eggs into a large bowl, add 1 cup of the sugar, and beat until stiff and creamy. Put the butter and milk into a saucepan and heat gently until the butter has melted. Meanwhile, arrange the apple slices in the buttered dish.

Gradually add the hot milk and butter to the egg mixture, beating well. Fold in the flour to make a smooth batter. Pour the mixture over the apples, then sprinkle with the remaining 1/4 cup sugar and the nutmeg. Bake in a preheated oven at 350°F for 20–25 minutes until puffed and golden. Serve hot or cold with heavy cream or vanilla ice cream.

THE MENU
FOR 8 PEOPLE

Baked Fennel with
Shallots and Spicy
Dressing

Lamb Navarin

Garlic and Parsley
Bread

Warm Chocolate
and Coffee Dessert

TO DRINK

Syrah (Shiraz),
Merlot, Cabernet
Sauvignon

2 fennel bulbs

4 shallots, chopped

1 teaspoon sugar

3 tablespoons olive oil

1 garlic clove, crushed
and chopped

1 inch fresh ginger,
peeled and chopped

a bunch of scallions,
sliced

1 tablespoon sesame oil

freshly squeezed juice of
1 lemon

1/2 teaspoon chile powder

sea salt and freshly
ground black pepper

serves 8

baked fennel with shallots and spicy dressing

Fennel is a beautiful vegetable, and very versatile. You can roast it with
other vegetables or serve raw in a salad, finely sliced or chopped. The
fennel bulbs come in two shapes—very slim and tall, or plump and round.
Guess what: the slim ones are male and the plump ones female!

Cut off the base of the fennel bulbs and trim the tops. Cut each bulb lengthwise into
4 and cut out the hard core. Put into an ovenproof dish and add the shallots, sugar,
and 2 tablespoons of the olive oil. Mix well and bake in a preheated oven at 325°F
for 30 minutes.

Put the remaining olive oil into a small saucepan, add the garlic and ginger, and cook
over very low heat for 10 minutes. Add the scallions, sesame oil, lemon juice, chile
powder, salt, and pepper. Gently bring to a simmer, then pour over the roasted fennel,
mix well, and serve with all the juices.

warming winter supper

the scene

Lazy suppers of rich and comforting food can
banish all thoughts of beaches and bikinis. So
indulge in this menu of warming, slow-cooked
dishes, just perfect for the long winter evenings.
I call it comfort food.

the style

This simple supper needs a table with a
comfortable and country feel, so put out chunky
place mats, farmhouse china, and traditional
flatware. This is humble and wholesome eating
at its best.

lamb navarin

A fantastic dish that can be made in advance, then just finished off on the day: this makes your life easier and also improves the flavor of the dish. All the vegetables can be altered to suit your taste: try leeks, cauliflower and broccoli florets, asparagus, parsnips, turnips, pumpkin, or sweet potatoes—the list is endless.

4 lb. boneless leg or shoulder of lamb, cubed

3 tablespoons olive oil

3 tablespoons all-purpose flour

1 quart vegetable stock

2 cans chopped tomatoes, 15 oz. each, about 4 cups

1 tablespoon tomato purée

⅔ cup red wine

2 bay leaves

2 sprigs of marjoram

½ teaspoon paprika

2 garlic cloves, crushed and chopped

8 shallots

10 oz. baby carrots, scrubbed

10 oz. new potatoes, scrubbed

3 celery stalks, cut into chunks

4 oz. runner beans, chopped

2 oz. curly kale or other greens, coarsely chopped

sea salt and freshly ground black pepper

serves 8

THE WORK PLAN

the day before

- Prepare the lamb up to the point specified in the recipe. Cover and chill.
- Make the chocolate and coffee dessert and sauce, cover, and chill.

on the day

- Make the spicy dressing.

just before serving

- Reheat the lamb, add the vegetables, and finish cooking.
- Cook the fennel.
- Make the garlic bread.
- Reheat the dessert and sauce (in the microwave if you have one—the dessert for 6–7 minutes on Medium, the sauce for 3 minutes on Medium).

Trim any excess fat from the lamb. Heat the oil in a large, flameproof casserole or saucepan, add the lamb, and cook briefly until browned all over. Depending on the size of the pan, you may have to do this in batches.

Return all the meat to the pan, sprinkle with a fine dusting of flour, mix well, and repeat until all the flour has been incorporated. Add the vegetable stock, tomatoes, tomato purée, wine, herbs, paprika, garlic, and shallots. Mix well and bring to a boil. Reduce the heat and simmer gently for 1 hour, stirring from time to time. Add salt and pepper to taste. (If making in advance, prepare up to this point, let cool, then chill overnight.) Add the carrots, potatoes, and celery and cook for 15 minutes. Add the beans and curly kale or greens and stir gently. Cover with a lid and cook for a further 5 minutes, then serve with the garlic and parsley bread.

garlic and parsley bread

Everyone loves this easy bread, ideal for mopping up all those juices. It can be made with other breads, so choose your family favorite.

3–4 garlic cloves, finely chopped

a bunch of flat-leaf parsley, chopped

½ teaspoon hot red pepper flakes

olive oil

sea salt and freshly ground black pepper

2 loaves ciabatta bread, split lengthwise

serves 8

Sprinkle the garlic, parsley, pepper flakes, salt, and pepper evenly over the opened bread halves. Drizzle generously with olive oil, then cook under a preheated broiler until golden. Cut the bread into chunks and serve at once with the lamb navarin.

warm chocolate and coffee dessert

This dessert can be made in advance, then just reheated on the day. Don't scrimp on the chocolate sauce ingredients: they make a thick, rich, and glossy sauce that will become one of your prized favorites. You can also serve it with poached pears, ice cream, or other desserts.

1 teaspoon instant coffee

1¾ sticks butter

1 cup minus
2 tablespoons sugar

2 large eggs

1½ cups all-purpose
flour

milk, as needed

½ cup unsweetened
cocoa powder

light cream, to serve

CHOCOLATE SAUCE

4 squares (4 oz.)
bittersweet chocolate

1 stick butter

¼ cup sugar

¾ cup heavy cream

*a plum pudding mold,
1 quart, buttered*

*foil, buttered, or
parchment paper*

serves 8

Put the coffee into a cup, stir in 1 teaspoon boiling water, and stir to dissolve. Put 4 inches water into a saucepan large enough to hold the bowl. Put the butter and sugar into a mixing bowl and, using an electric beater, beat until creamy, light, and very pale. Beat in the eggs and coffee.

Sift in the flour and cocoa powder and fold into the butter mixture using a large metal spoon, adding a little milk if the mixture seems very stiff. Transfer to the prepared pudding mold and cover tightly with the buttered foil or wax paper. Put into the saucepan of water, cover with a lid, and bring to a boil. Reduce the heat and simmer for 1½ hours, checking the water level from time to time. Remove the mold from the saucepan and carefully turn out the dessert onto a large plate. Serve hot or warm with the chocolate sauce and light cream.

To make the sauce, put the chocolate, butter, sugar, and cream into a small saucepan. Heat gently, stirring frequently, until melted. Remove from the heat and set aside until ready to serve.

THE MENU

FOR 4 PEOPLE

**Rich Root Soup
with Green Tarragon
Drizzle**

**Poached Mushrooms
with Egg Noodles**

**Roasted Butternut
Squash, Red Onions,
Baby Potatoes, and
Fennel with
Chickpeas
in Tomato Sauce**

Parmesan Cookies

**Blackberry and
Apple Pie with
Real Custard**

TO DRINK

**Sauvignon Blanc,
Gamay**

country vegetarian lunch

the scene

Easy, relaxed, low-key entertaining with really good friends means the chatter and laughter will flow. This menu is a celebration of garden or market produce, using beautiful, colorful vegetables just bursting with life and flavor. Get back to nature and enjoy the bounty of the countryside.

the style

Think farmers' market or kitchen garden, then keep the rustic look and extend it to your table. This isn't the time to worry about matching plates or neat presentation—use mixed china and chunky utensils and gather flowers and herbs from the garden to add to that country feeling.

THE WORK PLAN

the day before

- Make the soup and tomato sauce, cover, and chill.
- Make the dough, wrap, and chill.
- Make the Parmesan cookies and store in an airtight container.

on the day

- Assemble and cook the pie.
- Make the custard and cover with plastic wrap.

just before serving

- Prepare and roast the vegetables.
- Make the poached mushrooms.
- Make the tarragon drizzle.
- Reheat the tomato sauce.
- Reheat the custard.

rich root soup with green tarragon drizzle

In the cold of the winter, a thick, rich soup is a delight every time—serve it with lots of warm, freshly baked bread and cold butter. The tarragon drizzle transforms this rather comforting, old-fashioned soup into something stylish and modern!

Put the oil into a large saucepan, heat gently, add the onion, garlic, and celery, and cook for 5 minutes. Add the parsnip, rutabaga, and carrot and cook for 3 minutes. Mix the bouillon powder with 1 1/2 quarts boiling water and add to the vegetables. Add salt and pepper to taste, bring to a boil, and simmer for 35 minutes, until the vegetables are tender. Remove from the heat and blend until smooth.

To make the drizzle, put the tarragon into a bowl and add the lemon juice and oil. Using a stick blender, blend until smooth. Ladle the hot soup into bowls, add a swirl of tarragon drizzle, and serve.

1 tablespoon olive oil

2 onions, chopped

1 garlic clove, chopped

3 celery stalks, chopped

1 lb. parsnips, chopped

1 lb. rutabagas, chopped

1 lb. carrots, chopped

3 1/2 teaspoons good-quality vegetable bouillon powder

sea salt and freshly ground black pepper

GREEN TARRAGON DRIZZLE

a bunch of tarragon, finely chopped

freshly squeezed juice of 1/2 lemon

1/4 cup olive oil

serves 4

poached mushrooms with egg noodles

The purity and natural flavors of this noodle dish will make you feel very healthy! Using tofu or perhaps chicken breast, instead of mushrooms, is also delicious.

4 cremini mushrooms

4 scallions, trimmed

4 shallots

2 bay leaves

8 oz. dried egg noodles

2 zucchini, sliced into rounds

4 oz. baby sweet corn, trimmed

4 oz. runner beans or Chinese yard-long beans, sliced

4 oz. spinach, washed and chopped, about 1 cup

1 tablespoon soy sauce

sea salt and freshly ground black pepper

Serves 4

Put the mushrooms into a large saucepan and add the scallions, shallots, bay leaves, salt, and pepper. Add water to cover and heat until simmering. Cover with a lid and cook for 20 minutes. Add the noodles to the pan of vegetables, adding extra water to cover if necessary. Add the zucchini, sweet corn, beans, spinach and soy sauce. Simmer for a further 4 minutes, until the noodles and vegetables are cooked. Serve in bowls with a ladle of the cooking juices.

parmesan cookies

10 oz. Parmesan cheese, grated

a baking tray, lined with parchment paper

makes 20

Pile teaspoons of the grated Parmesan onto the lined baking tray and flatten gently to give equal rounds. Bake in a preheated oven at 375°F for 5 minutes. Remove the paper from the baking tray with the cookies still on it. Replace with another sheet of paper and repeat with the remaining cheese. Serve with the roasted vegetables.

roasted butternut squash, red onions, baby potatoes, and fennel with chickpeas in tomato sauce

An easy dish. The tomato sauce can be made the night before—in fact it actually improves overnight.

1 butternut squash or ½ pumpkin, cut into wedges, skin left on and seeds left in

3 small red onions, cut into wedges

8 baby new potatoes, halved

2 fennel bulbs, trimmed and cut into wedges

3 tablespoons olive oil

1 can chickpeas, 15 oz., drained and rinsed, about 2 cups

sea salt and freshly ground black pepper

TOMATO SAUCE

2 tablespoons olive oil

1 onion, chopped

2 celery stalks, chopped

1 leek, trimmed and chopped

1 garlic clove, chopped

1 can chopped tomatoes, 15 oz., about 2 cups

1 tablespoon tomato purée

½ cup red wine

sea salt and freshly ground black pepper

serves 4

Put the squash, onion, potato, and fennel into a roasting pan. Add the oil and sprinkle with salt and pepper. Toss to coat, then roast in a preheated oven at 400°F for 45 minutes, checking after 30 minutes that the vegetables are cooking evenly and turning them if needed. Add the chickpeas and roast for a further 5–10 minutes until all the vegetables are browned and tender.

To make the tomato sauce, heat the oil in a saucepan. Add the onion, celery, leek, and garlic and sauté for 5 minutes until soft. Add the tomatoes, tomato purée, and red wine. Simmer gently for 30 minutes, adding a little more red wine if the sauce becomes too thick. Using a stick blender, process until smooth. Add salt and pepper to taste, pour over the roasted vegetables, and serve with the Parmesan cookies.

blackberry and apple pie

For the best results, always use a metal pie dish: it will get hotter than ceramic and guarantees to cook the pie crust until dry and crumbly rather than soggy.

DOUGH

2¹/₃ cups
all-purpose flour

2 sticks butter, cut into small pieces

¹/₂ cup minus
1 tablespoon sugar,
plus extra for
sprinkling

3–4 egg yolks

milk, for brushing

FILLING

1¹/₂ lb. baking
apples, cored,
peeled, and sliced

1 lb. blackberries,
about 3¹/₂ cups

¹/₂ cup sugar

real custard (below,
right), to serve

*a metal pie pan,
10 inches diameter,
lightly buttered*

serves 4

Put the flour and butter into a food processor and process until the mixture looks like bread crumbs. Add the sugar and process briefly. With the machine running, gradually add 3 egg yolks until the mixture comes together to form a ball. (Add the extra egg yolk if it is too dry.) Transfer the dough to a lightly floured surface and knead very gently with your hands until smooth. Divide in half, wrap each piece in plastic wrap, and chill for 40 minutes.

Remove 1 piece of chilled dough from the refrigerator and roll out until just larger than the pie pan. Put the rolled dough into the pie pan pressing the base and rim gently to push out any air bubbles. Layer the apple slices, blackberries, and sugar over the dough, piling the fruit high, then brush milk over the dough rim.

Roll out the remaining dough to just bigger than the dish and drape it over the fruit, taking care not to stretch it. Trim the excess dough away from the edge and then go around the rim of the pie, pinching the dough together with your fingers to seal. Using a small, sharp knife, cut a vent in the middle of the pie to let the steam escape.

Brush the top of the pie all over with milk and sprinkle generously with sugar. Bake in a preheated oven at 425°F for 30 minutes, then reduce to 350°F and cook for about another 30 minutes until golden. Serve hot with custard.

real custard

It takes a little time and patience, and a very gentle heat, to make this custard so rich and glossy—but it's worth it. Don't try to hurry, or the eggs will scramble.

2 vanilla beans

1¹/₂ cups milk

1 cup heavy cream

¹/₃ cup sugar

4 extra-large egg yolks

serves 4

Split the vanilla beans in half lengthwise and scrape out the seeds. Put the milk, cream, sugar, and vanilla seeds into a saucepan and heat gently until just before boiling point, then reduce the heat to low. Put the egg yolks into a bowl and beat until frothy. Add a little of the hot milk mixture to the eggs and beat again. Pour the egg yolk mixture into the saucepan and beat again. Cook over very low heat, stirring constantly with a wooden spoon, until the custard thickens, about 6 minutes. Serve.

weekend dining

the scene

Weekend dining is always special to me. Weekdays are often rushed, but at last, on the weekend, there's time for cooking at home with ease. I love being in the kitchen, slowly preparing a great meal, the radio on, maybe glancing through the newspaper, catching up on a few small kitchen tasks. As the food is roasted, it gradually fills the house with warmth and delicious aromas.

the style

Happy chaos catering for all ages and needs, so let your children set the table and gather all that's needed. There is something traditional about a roast lunch, so it's a good time to wheel out bone-handled flatware and family heirloom china.

THE MENU

FOR 8 PEOPLE

Sage and Stilton Flatbread

Roast Rib of Beef with Horseradish Yorkshire Puddings

Roast Potatoes and Parsnips

Carrot and Spinach Butter Mash

Vin Santo Trifle

TO DRINK

Syrah (Shiraz), Merlot, Cabernet Sauvignon

THE WORK PLAN

the day before

- Make the trifle, cover, and chill.

on the day

- Preheat the oven until hot.
- Prepare the beef, calculate the cooking time, and put into the preheated oven.
- Make the flatbread and serve with pre-lunch drinks.
- Parboil the potatoes and transfer to the oven to roast. Parboil the parsnips (reserving the water), drain, and set aside.
- Cook the carrots (reserving the water), drain, and keep them warm in the oven.
- Add the parsnips to the potatoes, to roast.
- Prepare and cook the Yorkshire puddings.
- Remove the beef from the oven and keep it warm while you make the gravy and cook the Yorkshire puddings.
- Mash the carrots, add the spinach, and cook while someone carves the beef.

sage and stilton flatbread

Make this as an appetizer to serve with drinks when your friends and family arrive. If Stilton is not your favorite cheese, try using another blue cheese such as Roquefort or Gorgonzola, brie, or a hard cheese such as mature Cheddar.

1 lb. all-purpose flour

1 teaspoon baking powder

1 cup plain yogurt

1 stick butter, melted

2 eggs, beaten

3 tablespoons chopped fresh sage

4 oz. Stilton cheese, crumbled

a baking tray, lightly oiled

serves 8

Sift the flour and baking powder into a bowl and make a well in the middle. Put the yogurt, melted butter, eggs, and sage into a separate bowl and mix. Pour the mixture into the well in the flour and stir with a wooden spoon until well blended.

Knead the dough into a ball, put onto the prepared baking tray, and roll out to a 12-inch disk. Cook in a preheated oven at 350°F for 20 minutes. Remove, crumble the Stilton over the top, and return to the oven for a further 10 minutes. Remove and let cool a little before removing from the tray. Transfer to a chopping board, cut into wedges, and serve.

roast prime rib

When winter closes in, I always want to cook this meal, perfect for a large, happy gathering around a table ringing with laughter and good stories. To make carving easier, ask the butcher to bone and roll the beef, but make sure you get the bones as well and roast them with the meat. They add to the flavor of the gravy (very important—without good gravy it's not a true roast!)

2 tablespoons all-purpose flour

2 teaspoons mustard powder

2 teaspoons freshly ground black pepper

3-bone rib roast, about 6 lb.

1 tablespoon oil

GRAVY

1 tablespoon all-purpose flour

reserved cooking water from the vegetables

a splash of Worcestershire sauce

sea salt and freshly ground black pepper

serves 8

Put the flour, mustard powder, and pepper into a bowl, mix briefly, then rub the beef all over with the mixture. Heat the oil in a large roasting pan, add the beef, then put into a preheated oven at 400°F. After 20 minutes reduce the heat to 350°F and cook for a further 20 minutes per pound for rare, 25 minutes per pound for medium, and 30 minutes per pound for well done. Remove the beef from the oven and let rest for 20 minutes, while you make the Yorkshire puddings (right).

Remove the beef from the roasting pan. Drain off all but 2 tablespoons of the excess fat and reserve it to make the Yorkshire puddings. To make the gravy, add the flour to the fat in the pan and stir to form a paste. Put on top of the stove over high heat and gradually add the vegetable water, stirring and scraping up all the residue from the roasting pan, until you have a good gravy consistency. Bring to a boil and add salt, pepper, and a splash of Worcestershire sauce. Pour into a sauceboat and keep it warm until ready to serve.

horseradish yorkshire puddings

The secret of Yorkshire puddings is to have the oven hot and to preheat the oil in the pan. Cook them only when everyone is ready and everything is organized and under control in the kitchen—if they are not eaten at once, they will deflate and lose their crunch.

1/2 cup all-purpose flour

1 egg

1/3 cup milk

1 teaspoon grated fresh horseradish

4 tablespoons lard or beef drippings from the roast rib of beef

sea salt and freshly ground black pepper

a 12-cup muffin pan

serves 8

Sift the flour into a bowl and make a well in the middle. Put the egg, milk, horseradish, and 1/4 cup water into a separate bowl, add a pinch of salt and pepper, and mix. Slowly pour the mixture into the well in the flour, beating with an electric beater or a wooden spoon until you have a smooth batter.

While the beef is resting out of the oven, increase the oven temperature to 425°F. Divide the lard between 8 of the muffin cups and heat the pan in the oven for 10 minutes. Remove and fill the 8 cups with batter. Cook on the top rack of the oven for 8–10 minutes until puffed and golden.

roast potatoes and parsnips

When cooking roast potatoes, the oven should be very hot—hotter than for the beef. If you have a double oven, this is no problem, as the meat can be in one and the potatoes in another, but with a single oven you have to play around with the temperature and the position of the food. Increase the oven temperature, and cook the beef at the bottom of the oven and the potatoes at the top. You may need to reduce the cooking time for the beef, or remove it from the oven for 20 minutes before it is finished, keep it warm, and then return and continue to cook. It sounds tricky but really it's not— I call it oven juggling!

1 lb. potatoes, cut into equal pieces

1 lb. parsnips, cut into equal pieces

1/3 cup olive oil

sea salt

serves 8

Cook the potatoes in a saucepan of boiling, salted water for 12 minutes, drain well, and return them to the pan. Put over low heat for 2 minutes, to steam off the excess moisture. Cover with a lid and shake the pan vigorously a few times, to give the potatoes a floury coating. Add 1/4 cup of the oil and coat well.

Cook the parsnips in a saucepan of boiling, salted water for 8 minutes, then drain well, reserving the cooking water for the gravy. Add the remaining oil to the parsnips or rutabagas and shake to coat.

Put the potatoes into a large roasting pan and cook in a preheated oven at 425°F for 20 minutes. Add the parsnips and return to the oven for a further 15 minutes until crunchy and golden.

vin santo trifle

This trifle is just delicious but, instead of custard, I use a mixture of cream and mascarpone. Go to an Italian store for Vin Santo (a sweet wine) and biscotti (hard, almond-flavored Italian cookies). These are traditionally eaten dipped into the wine, but here make a splendid addition to trifle.

8 oz. Italian biscotti

1/2 cup Vin Santo wine

8 ripe figs, quartered lengthwise

1 can pitted cherries, 15 oz.

2 cups heavy cream

1 lb. mascarpone cheese

1/3 cup sugar

2 squares (2 oz.) white chocolate

1/2 cup slivered almonds

serves 8

Put the biscotti into a large serving bowl, preferably glass. Pour over the Vin Santo and arrange the figs and cherries on top. Put the cream into a bowl and whip lightly until soft peaks form. Add the mascarpone and sugar and continue whipping until stiff. Spoon the cream and mascarpone mixture over the fruit, then sprinkle with almonds. Using a vegetable peeler, make curls with the white chocolate and sprinkle over the trifle. Chill until needed.

carrot and spinach butter mash

1 lb. carrots, chopped

6 tablespoons butter

10 oz. spinach, chopped

sea salt and freshly ground black pepper

serves 8

Cook the carrots in a saucepan of boiling, salted water for 30 minutes, or until tender. Drain well, reserving the cooking water for the gravy. Return the carrots to the pan and put over low heat. Steam off the excess water, stirring frequently, for 2 minutes. Remove from the heat, add the butter, salt, and pepper, and mash well. Add the spinach and stir for 2 minutes, until wilted.

THE MENU

FOR 6 PEOPLE

Phyllo Spinach and
Ricotta Pastries

Slow-Roasted
Tomatoes

Daube of Beef

or

Fish and Spring
Greens Pie

Panettone Bread
and Butter
Pudding
with Plums

TO DRINK

Merlot for the
Beef, Zinfandel or
Gamay for the
Fish Pie

THE WORK PLAN

two days before

- Marinate the beef, cover, and chill overnight.

the day before

- Cook the daube of beef. Remove from the oven, let cool, then chill overnight.

on the day

- Prepare but do not cook the phyllo pastries, put onto the baking tray, cover, and chill.
- Prepare but do not cook the fish pie, cover with plastic wrap, and chill.
- Prepare but do not cook the bread and butter pudding, cover, and chill.

just before serving

- Cook the phyllo pastries.
- Reheat the daube of beef or cook the fish pie.
- Cook the bread and butter pudding.
- Cook pasta or potatoes to serve with the beef.

dinner in advance

the scene

We all lead busy lives, and sometimes we invite friends over and then find we are snowed under with work—we've all been there! But this is a totally prepare-in-advance menu with just the simplest last-minute cooking, so you can rush home late and still serve a stunning meal.

the style

A setting to match the cook—calm and unflustered. As time is short, you can set the table the night before, or even in the morning, but really it should be simple and casual. Your guests should be welcomed by the sight of a serene cook and table, then a happy, easy meal will follow naturally.

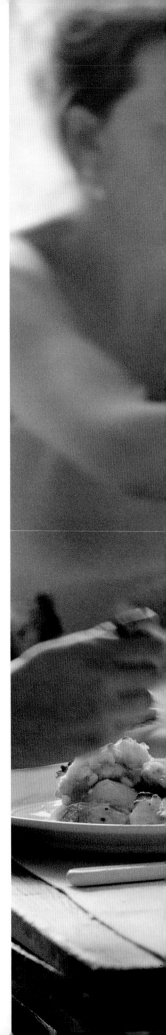

phyllo, spinach, and ricotta pastries

These delicious little packages of spinach and creamy ricotta encased in crisp phyllo are originally from Morocco, but these days they can be found all around the Mediterranean, with countless variations.

12 oz. baby spinach, washed and dried, 3 cups

6 oz. phyllo pastry dough

4 tablespoons butter, melted

8 oz. fresh ricotta cheese, about 1 cup

½ cup pine nuts, toasted in a dry skillet

sea salt and freshly ground black pepper

serves 6

Put the spinach into a large saucepan over medium heat. Cook, stirring, until all the leaves have wilted, about 5 minutes. Transfer to a large colander and let cool, while the excess liquid drips out.

Put a dish cloth onto a clean work surface and put a sheet of phyllo on top. Brush with melted butter and layer 3 more of the sheets on top, brushing each with butter. Put the ricotta, pine nuts, cooled spinach, salt, and pepper into a bowl and mix. Spread the mixture over the phyllo, leaving a 2-inch border all around.

Starting with the long side, roll up the phyllo into a log shape, using the cloth to help you roll. Lightly twist the ends to enclose. Brush all over with butter, transfer to a baking tray, and cook in a preheated oven at 350°F for 30 minutes until golden. Slice and serve with the slow-roasted tomatoes.

slow-roasted tomatoes

6 tomatoes, halved crosswise

serves 6

Put the tomato halves, skin side down, into an ovenproof dish, spacing them so that they do not touch. Cook in a preheated oven at 250°F for 2 hours. Serve with the phyllo pastries.

daube of beef

This dish must be made in advance in order for the flavors to develop and the sauce to taste rich and delicious. If you are reheating it from cold, put into a preheated oven at 350°F for 35 minutes. Serve with egg noodle pasta, tossed in parsley and butter, or with boiled potatoes.

4 lb. boneless rump roast

1 bottle white wine, 750 ml

2 bay leaves

1/4 cup olive oil

2 onions, sliced

2 garlic cloves, chopped

3 tablespoons all-purpose flour, plus extra for dusting

1 tablespoon drained capers

4 oz. black olives, such as niçoise or kalamata, pitted, about 1 cup

1 can chopped tomatoes, 15 oz., about 2 cups

grated zest of 1/2 orange

8 oz. baby carrots

4 oz. button mushrooms

a large bunch of flat-leaf parsley, chopped

sea salt and freshly ground black pepper

serves 6

Put the beef, wine, bay leaves, salt, and pepper into a large bowl, cover, and chill for 24 hours, turning the beef in its marinade from time to time.

Drain the beef, reserving the marinade, and pat dry with paper towels. Heat 2 tablespoons of the oil in a large flameproof casserole, add the onions and garlic, and cook gently for 8 minutes. Sprinkle with the flour and stir. Add the marinade liquid a little at a time, stirring constantly. Add the capers, olives, tomatoes, and orange zest and simmer while you prepare the beef.

Put the remaining 2 tablespoons olive oil into a skillet and heat until hot. Dust the beef with flour and add to the skillet. Sauté until brown on all sides, then transfer to the casserole. Put a few tablespoons of juice from the casserole back into the skillet and stir to scrape up any meaty bits. Add the juice and bits back to the casserole.

Cover with a lid, transfer to a preheated oven at 275°F, and cook for 2 hours. Remove from the oven and add the carrots and mushrooms. Return the casserole to the oven and cook for another hour.

Remove the beef to a board, slice thickly, and serve on heated dinner plates. Stir the chopped parsley into the sauce and spoon the sauce and vegetables over the beef.

Nothing beats a good daube of beef, and this one is perfect, because it's mine! The meat is tender, the juices rich, and vegetables succulent.

fish and spring greens pie

Everyone loves a creamy fish pie, packed with goodness.

1 lb. white fish fillet, such as cod, haddock, or halibut

1 lb. trout fillet

8 oz. uncooked shrimp, peeled

4 oz. scallops

10 oz. greens or Savoy cabbage, coarsely chopped

2 lb. potatoes, cut into equal pieces

4 tablespoons butter

1/2 cup milk

sea salt and freshly ground black pepper

SAUCE

2 cups milk

1 stick butter

1/3 cup all-purpose flour

4 oz. Cheddar cheese, grated

sea salt and freshly ground black pepper

serves 6

Dry the fish and seafood thoroughly with paper towels. Arrange the greens in a large ovenproof dish and put the fish and seafood on top.

Cook the potatoes in a saucepan of boiling, salted water for 20 minutes, or until tender when pierced with a knife. Drain and return to the pan. Mash well, then add the butter, milk, salt, and pepper. Beat well with a wooden spoon, then set aside until needed.

To make the sauce, put the milk into a small saucepan and heat gently until warm. Melt the butter in a separate saucepan and add the flour. Remove from the heat, stir, return to the heat, then add a little of the warm milk. Stir well, then gradually stir in the remaining warm milk until the sauce is smooth. Add the cheese, salt, and pepper, then pour over the fish.

Spoon the mashed potatoes evenly over the top, giving it a scalloped effect. If you want a more traditional look, run a fork over the surface of the potato. Transfer to a preheated oven at 400°F and bake for 20 minutes, then reduce to 325°F and cook for a further 25 minutes.

One of my comfort foods is fish pie. The velvety sauce, the creamy mashed potato—it's a dish I revisit time and again.

panettone bread and butter pudding with plums

Traditional bread and butter pudding, with creamy custard and plump raisins, is wonderful. I think it's even better with rich Italian panettone and juicy blush-colored plums.

6 slices panettone or other sweet bread, spread with butter

6 ripe plums, halved, pitted, and sliced

1¼ cups milk

½ cup heavy cream

¼ cup sugar

3 large eggs

a baking dish, enamel if possible, buttered

serves 6

Cut the slices of buttered panettone in half and put a few slices of plum on top. Arrange in an overlapping layer in the baking dish.

Put the milk, cream, sugar, and eggs into a bowl and beat well. Pour the mixture over the panettone and plums. Chop any remaining plum slices into small pieces and sprinkle over the top. Set aside for 1 hour to let the panettone soak up the creamy liquid.

Cook in a preheated oven at 350°F for 35 minutes. Serve warm.

THE WORK PLAN

the day before

- Make the orange and lemon bake, cover, and store in a cool place.
- Prepare the pork fillet, cover, and chill.

on the day

- Make the lime and soy dressing for the tuna, cover, and chill.
- Roast the bell peppers and cook the lentils.
- Make the minted yogurt.
- Make the scallion dressing for the pork, cover, and chill.
- Cook the potatoes and beans, drain, and set aside.

just before serving

- Cook the pork.
- Assemble the salad.
- Prepare the endive and watercress for the salad.
- Sear the tuna.

summer sundown

the scene

At the end of a hot summer's day, relax in the garden and enjoy this fresh and tangy menu full of seasonal produce. Outdoor eating is a real treat for all, so if you have a garden or a terrace, use it.

the style

Pretty and romantic, just keep it easy and calm so that it doesn't detract from the beauty of your surroundings. Use soft colors with informal china to create a warm and relaxed table so you can enjoy the food and the view.

seared tuna salad with lime and soy dressing

Tuna is such a popular fish today and with the availability of such fresh quality, it is a joy to cook and eat.

10 oz. fresh tuna steak

grated zest and freshly squeezed juice of 2 limes, plus extra wedges, to serve

1 chile, finely chopped

1/3 cup light soy sauce

2 kaffir lime leaves, finely sliced

1 stalk of lemongrass, very finely sliced

3 tablespoons olive oil

3 Belgian endive, leaves separated

2 bunches of watercress

sea salt and freshly ground black pepper

serves 8

Heat a stove-top grill pan until very hot, then add the tuna steak. Cook for 2–3 minutes on each side. Don't move it around before this or it will not have formed a good crust and will break up. Remove to a carving board and let rest.

To make the dressing, put the lime zest and juice into a bowl. Add the chile, soy sauce, lime leaves, lemongrass, oil, salt, and pepper. Arrange the endive leaves on serving plates. Cut the tuna crosswise into fine slices and arrange on top of the salad. Add the watercress and wedges of lime, spoon the dressing over the top, and serve.

Use brown lentils for salads—they have a delicious, earthy flavor.

sage-stuffed pork fillet with lentils and scallion dressing

This meal would be fit to serve in many restaurants and yet is very simple. Pork tenderloin is quick and easy to cook. People seem to worry a great deal about pork being undercooked or tough, but follow the instructions and it will always be cooked through and moist.

2 pork tenderloins, about 14 oz. each

leaves from a large bunch of sage

8 thin slices prosciutto

8 oz. brown lentils, about 1½ cups

6 scallions, sliced

3 tablespoons olive oil

1 tablespoon red wine

½ cup sour cream

1 lb. roasted red bell peppers in a bottle, drained and cut into strips

a bunch of chives, chopped

sea salt and freshly ground black pepper

serves 8

Trim the pork of any excess fat and, using a long, thin knife, pierce each tenderloin lengthwise through the middle. Push the sage leaves into the slit and, using the handle of a wooden spoon, push them further along the slit. Sprinkle the fillets with salt and pepper, then wrap each one in 4 slices of prosciutto. Brush a roasting pan with oil, add the wrapped tenderloins, and cook in a preheated oven at 350°F for 35 minutes. Remove, let rest for 5 minutes, then cut into 1-inch slices.

Meanwhile, cook the lentils in simmering water for 20 minutes until tender, then drain. Put the scallions into a bowl, add the oil, wine, and sour cream, and mix. Add the bell peppers to the drained lentils and spoon onto serving plates. Top with the pork slices, scallion dressing, and chives, then serve.

new potato, garden pea, and bean salad

A wonderful combination of summer ingredients, bursting with fresh vegetable flavors. If fresh peas aren't available, use frozen instead.

3 lb. new potatoes

10 oz. shelled peas, 2 cups

10 oz. runner beans

2 garlic cloves, chopped

⅓ cup olive oil

2 tablespoons Dijon mustard

freshly squeezed juice of 1 lemon

sea salt and freshly ground black pepper

leaves from a bunch of flat-leaf parsley, to serve

serves 8

Cook the potatoes in boiling, salted water for 20 minutes or until tender, then drain and set aside. Cook the peas and runner beans together in boiling, salted water for 4 minutes. Drain and refresh in changes of cold water until cool, then drain again.

Put the garlic into a small bowl and add the oil, mustard, lemon juice, salt, and pepper. Cut the potatoes in half and put into a large bowl. Stir in the peas and beans. Just before serving, add the dressing, toss well, and sprinkle with parsley.

4 large eggs

1/2 cup sugar

1 1/4 cups unsweetened shredded coconut

4 tablespoons softened butter

1 cup ground almonds or 1 1/4 cups slivered almonds, ground to a meal in a blender

grated zest and freshly squeezed juice of 2 unwaxed lemons

grated zest and juice of 2 oranges

1/2 cup milk

1/3 cup self-rising flour

MINTED YOGURT

1 cup plain yogurt

a bunch of mint, finely chopped

a pie pan, 8 inches diameter, buttered

serves 8

orange and lemon bake with minted yogurt

This is a mixture of things that I love—sponge cake, coconut, ground almonds, and citrus fruits.

To make the bake, put the eggs, sugar, coconut, butter, ground almonds, lemon and orange zest and juice, milk, and self-rising flour into a food processor and process for 1 minute until blended. Transfer the mixture to the buttered pan and bake in a preheated oven at 350°F for 45 minutes until golden brown. Remove from the oven and let cool.

Put the yogurt into a bowl and add the mint. Mix well and serve spooned over the bake.

THE MENU

FOR 4 PEOPLE

Stuffed Sweet Peppers

Country Chicken

Pasta Ribbons with Parsley

Lemon Polenta Cake
with Pouring Cream

TO DRINK

Light beer, Pinot Blanc,
Sauvignon Blanc

supper on a budget

the scene

It's not always necessary or possible to spend large amounts of money when cooking for friends. This simple yet delicious menu has been devised with a low budget in mind. It's the sort of supper that you would serve to a small gathering of good friends for an after-work, relaxed, easy meal with the emphasis on simplicity. This is the ideal meal for two couples—it won't cost the earth, but still tastes and looks delicious.

the style

Easy comfort is what this meal is all about, so carry this idea through to the table. Pull up a small, low table in front of the fire with pillows to sit on, and put piles of plates, napkins, knives, and forks on the table for people to help themselves. Serve wine or beer—and feel the fire warm your heart.

stuffed sweet peppers

Long, thin, sweet Cubanelle peppers are best for this dish. However, if they aren't in season, ordinary bell peppers can be used, though a little extra filling may be needed, as they tend to be larger.

4 Cubanelle peppers, halved lengthwise and seeded	3 oz. olives stuffed with anchovies, chopped
8 oz. mushrooms, coarsely chopped	1/2 tablespoon paprika
5 oz. mozzarella cheese, drained and cut into large dice	sea salt and freshly ground black pepper
2 garlic cloves, chopped	*a baking tray, lightly oiled*
3 tablespoons olive oil	serves 4

Put the pepper halves skin side down onto the oiled baking tray.

Put the mushrooms, mozzarella, garlic, oil, olives, and paprika into a bowl. Add salt and pepper to taste and mix well. Spoon the mixture into the peppers. Cook near the top of a preheated oven at 350°F for 30 minutes. Serve hot or warm.

country chicken

If you don't fancy cutting up a whole chicken, ask the butcher to do it for you, or simply buy chicken pieces.

Put the chicken pieces into a bowl and add the shallots, bay leaves, bacon, oil, salt, and pepper. Mix well, transfer to a roasting pan, and cook in a preheated oven at 350°F for 30 minutes.

Put the mustard into a small bowl, then stir in the tarragon and wine. Remove the chicken from the oven and pour off any excess fat. Pour the mustard and tarragon mixture over the chicken and return it to the oven for a further 10 minutes. Serve with the pasta ribbons.

1 chicken, about 4 lb., cut into 8 pieces

8 shallots

5 bay leaves

8 oz. thick-cut bacon, chopped

2 tablespoons olive oil

1½ tablespoons whole-grain mustard

a bunch of tarragon, coarsely chopped

½ cup white wine

sea salt and freshly ground black pepper

serves 4

pasta ribbons with parsley

I love pappardelle pasta. Because of its extra width, whatever sauce you add, it will cling more easily and thus give more flavor.

Cook the pasta in a large saucepan of boiling, salted water until *al dente*, or according to the instructions on the package.

Drain the pasta well and return it to the pan, off the heat. Add the parsley, garlic, oil, lemon juice, salt and pepper. Toss well, then serve.

14 oz. dried pappardelle pasta

a bunch of flat-leaf parsley, coarsely chopped

1 garlic clove, finely chopped

¼ cup olive oil

freshly squeezed juice of ½ lemon

sea salt and freshly ground black pepper

serves 4

the day before

- Make the lemon polenta cake, let cool, then cover and store at room temperature. If serving hot, put the dish into a tray of water (to stop it drying out) and transfer to a preheated oven for 10 minutes at 300°F. Alternatively, reheat in the microwave for 6–7 minutes on Medium.
- Cut the chicken into pieces if whole and put into a bowl with the marinade ingredients. Cover and chill overnight.

just before serving

- Transfer the chicken to the roasting pan and put into the oven to cook.
- Make the tarragon and mustard mixture for the chicken.
- Prepare and cook the sweet peppers.
- Cook the pasta, chop the parsley and garlic.

lemon polenta cake with pouring cream

Remove the butter from the refrigerator 30 minutes before starting this recipe: when softer, it's easier to mix.

1½ sticks butter, cut into pieces

1¼ cups sugar

4 large eggs

3 unwaxed lemons

¾ cup Italian polenta or yellow cornmeal

¾ cup self-rising flour

1¼ cups light cream, to serve

an ovenproof dish, 8 inches diameter, lightly buttered

serves 4

Put the butter into a mixing bowl, add the sugar, and beat until creamy and smooth. Beat in the eggs one at a time (the mixture may separate, but will come back together when the flour is added).

Grate the zest and squeeze the juice from 2½ of the lemons. Slice the remaining lemon half and set aside. Add the lemon zest and juice to the cake mixture and mix well. Add the polenta or cornmeal and flour, fold in until evenly blended, then spoon into the buttered dish. Arrange the reserved lemon slices around the cake.

Bake in a preheated oven at 350°F for 25 minutes. Reduce to 325°F and cook for a further 10 minutes, until it is coming away from the edges of the dish and a knife inserted in the center comes out clean. Serve hot or at room temperature, with a pitcher of cream.

shrimp noodle broth

If, like me, you love a fiery heat, leave
the seeds in the chiles.

1 tablespoon vegetable oil

1 onion, sliced

4 inches fresh ginger or galangal,
peeled and sliced

2 garlic cloves, sliced

2 red chiles, seeded (optional) and sliced

1¼ lb. uncooked jumbo shrimp, peeled

2 quarts vegetable stock

1¼ lb. fresh udon noodles

a bunch of basil, preferably Thai basil,
coarsely chopped

a bunch of cilantro, coarsely chopped

serves 8

Heat the oil in a saucepan and add the
onion, ginger or galangal, garlic, and chiles.
Stir well and cook for 5 minutes over low
heat. Add the shrimp and cook for a further
2 minutes, then add the stock. Bring to a
boil, add the noodles, and cook for a
further 2 minutes. Stir the basil and
cilantro into the broth and serve.

fab fish lunch

the scene

The beauty of fish calls for simplicity, but these dishes can all be dressed up or down to suit any occasion.

the style

Serve from big vessels to enhance that look of the sea's bounty. Let everyone help themselves to more whenever they feel like it.

THE WORK PLAN

the day before

- Make the chowder, but don't add the cream and herbs. Cover and chill.
- Prepare the smoking pan, fillet the trout, and wrap it in prosciutto.
- Roll, tie, and smoke the trout. Let cool, cover, and chill.
- Make the lime mousse and lemon sauce.

on the day

- Make the shrimp noodle broth, but don't add the shrimp or noodles.
- Make the fish stew up to the point of adding herbs.

just before serving

- Make the cucumber salad. Slice the trout and cook on the grill pan.
- Finish all the above dishes to serve.

THE MENU
SERVES 8

Shrimp Noodle Broth

Smoked Fish Chowder

Tea-Smoked Trout with Cucumber Salad

Easy Fish Stew

Lime Mousse with Lemon Sauce

TO DRINK

Gewüztraminer, Pinot Grigio, Semillon

smoked fish chowder

This recipe is just perfect for damp and cold days—it will warm and satisfy everyone. Smoked haddock is produced on the East Coast but, if unavailable, use 7 oz. fresh haddock or cod plus 3 oz. smoked salmon to give the smoky flavor.

Heat the butter in a large saucepan. Add the leeks and bacon and cook for 5 minutes, but do not brown. Add the fish stock and bring to a simmer. Add the corn, potatoes, and fish and cook for 10 minutes. Add salt and pepper to taste and bring to a gentle boil. Just before serving, add the parsley, chives, and cream. Serve with thick slices of warm bread.

4 tablespoons butter

2 leeks, finely sliced

4 oz. bacon, chopped

2¾ cups fish stock

4 oz. canned corn, drained and rinsed, about ½ cup

4 oz. potatoes, cut into small cubes

10 oz. smoked haddock, skinned (see recipe introduction, left)

1 tablespoon chopped, fresh flat-leaf parsley

1 tablespoon chopped chives

½ cup heavy cream

sea salt and freshly ground black pepper

thick slices of bread, to serve

serves 8

tea-smoked trout with cucumber salad

This takes a little time, but for that special occasion is well worth it, as the flavor is so different. I love the way the fillets are rolled together, then tied and cut to give you a boneless slice of fish. An unusual treat.

3 oz. oak wood shavings

1 tablespoon jasmine tea

1 whole trout, about 4 lb., filleted and skinned

12 slices prosciutto

2 tablespoons sesame oil

CUCUMBER SALAD

2 cucumbers, peeled and halved lengthwise

grated zest and freshly squeezed juice of 2 limes

sea salt and freshly ground black pepper

an old roasting pan, lined with foil

a wire rack

serves 8

Sprinkle the wood shavings and tea into the lined roasting pan and mix well. Put a wire rack that fits the pan on top.

Put both trout fillets onto a cutting board, one on top of the other, top to tail. Shape with your hands into a long sausage. Wrap the prosciutto around the fillets, overlapping slightly, to cover completely. Tie pieces of kitchen twine around the trout at 2-inch intervals to secure, then cut into 8 thick slices. Rub the cut surfaces with sesame oil and transfer to the wire rack set over the roasting pan.

Completely cover the top of the pan with foil, making sure that it is sealed all the way around the edge to stop any smoke escaping. Put the pan over high heat for 10 minutes, moving it around from time to time, to ensure even smoking. Remove from the heat and let cool, covered, for 20 minutes.

To make the cucumber salad, scoop out the seeds from the peeled cucumber halves and discard. Finely slice the cucumber and put into a bowl. Add the lime zest and juice, salt, and pepper.

Heat a stove-top grill pan or a nonstick skillet until hot, add the smoked trout steaks, and cook for 3 minutes on each side. They should be brown and slightly crunchy on the outside. Remove and discard the twine and serve the fish with the cucumber salad.

easy fish stew

I love fish stew, and this easy, stress-free recipe makes a fantastic meal (I have used it many times). Don't forget to provide a few empty dishes for discarded shells and some bowls of warm water for washing fingers.

1/3 cup olive oil

3 garlic cloves, chopped

2 onions, chopped

2 leeks or onions, sliced

3 celery stalks, sliced

1 fennel bulb, trimmed and sliced

1 tablespoon all-purpose flour

1 bay leaf

a sprig of thyme

a generous pinch of saffron threads

3 cans chopped tomatoes, 15 oz. each, about 6 cups

2 quarts fish stock

2 lb. monkfish, cut into 8 pieces

1 lb. mussels in shells, scrubbed

8 scallops

8 uncooked shrimp, shell on

a bunch of flat-leaf parsley, chopped

sea salt and freshly ground black pepper

crusty bread, to serve

serves 8

Heat the oil in a large saucepan and add the garlic, onion, leeks, celery, and fennel. Cook over low to medium heat for 10 minutes until soft. Sprinkle in the flour and stir well. Add the bay leaf, thyme, saffron, tomatoes, fish stock, salt, and pepper. Bring to a boil, then simmer for 25 minutes. Add the monkfish, mussels, scallops, and shrimp, cover with a lid, and simmer very gently for 6 minutes. Remove from the heat and set aside, with the lid on, for 4 minutes. Add the parsley and serve with plenty of warm crusty bread.

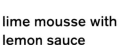

lime mousse with lemon sauce

Make this mousse the night before as there is nothing worse than willing an unset mousse to set before serving.

1 package (¼ oz.) powdered gelatin	**LEMON SAUCE**
3 eggs, separated	¼ cup sugar
⅓ cup sugar	thinly pared zest and freshly squeezed juice of 2 unwaxed lemons
grated zest and freshly squeezed juice of 3 limes	
⅔ cup heavy cream	serves 8

Put 3 tablespoons hot water into a small bowl and sprinkle in the gelatin. Put the bowl over a pan of simmering water for about 10 minutes. When completely dissolved, remove to room temperature and let cool a little.

Put the egg yolks and sugar into a large bowl and beat with an electric beater until thick and creamy. Add the lime zest and juice and beat well. Add the gelatin and beat again, then set aside for 5 minutes. Whisk the cream until soft peaks form, then fold into the lime mixture. Wash the beaters well and beat the egg whites until stiff. Add to the lime mixture and beat briefly. Spoon into individual pots or one serving bowl. Chill for at least 2 hours, or overnight.

To make the sauce, put the sugar, lemon juice, and half the zest into a small saucepan and mix. Bring to a boil, then simmer for 1 minute. Remove from the heat and cool completely to a syrupy sauce. If it is a little too thick, stir in a small amount of water. Sprinkle the remaining lemon zest over the mousse and serve with the sauce.

parties & celebrations

This is red-carpet dining. I love celebrating, and have been known to invent an occasion to be able to mark it with a special meal. Planning the reason, inviting friends, getting the look, choosing the menu and drinks, shopping, cooking, and then eating, drinking, and making merry. It's as happy and simple as that—so join me for a profusion of ideas and menus for that exciting celebration.

You don't have to be rich to be lavish and you can always cut corners. Don't invite too many people, especially if you don't have the space. Choose the menu according to your budget, and be prepared to adapt recipes (for example by using portobello mushrooms instead of porcini). Look out for wines as they appear on special offer and stock up.

Be organized. Make a list and work your way through it. Prepare as much of the food as possible in advance, set the table, and chill the drinks several hours before your guests arrive. Set out a tray with coffee and chocolates and get cocktails and glasses ready. Now go and have a refreshing shower, so that you look relaxed and happy to welcome your friends.

children's tea party

the scene

The birthday party is magical moment for every child, but it should also be fun for the parents. The most important thing to remember is not to over-cater—don't slave away in the kitchen, only to throw it all away because the children are just too excited to sit down and eat a healthy meal. They want treats—and at a party they should get them!

the style

Mini table and chairs with plates piled high. Use fun china for children with crazy designs, rather than plastic plates and cups. Balloons, of course!

cartwheel tortilla wraps

It's almost impossible to get children to eat something healthy at a birthday party, due to all the excitement, but don't give up. These wraps can be made the night before, then sliced just before the party, so removing some of the stress from Mommy!

3 flour tortillas
butter, for spreading
3 tablespoons cream cheese
1 large carrot, grated

serves 12

Put each tortilla flat onto a piece of plastic wrap, spread with butter and cream cheese, sprinkle with carrot, and roll up tightly, using the plastic wrap to help, and twisting the plastic wrap at either end. Chill for 2 hours to set, then cut into slices. Remove the plastic wrap and serve.

star and heart sandwiches

Choose a variety of breads—whole wheat, brown, rye, and white. Any shapes can be used, so let your artistic side run wild.

24 slices bread, a mixture of brown and white, buttered

FILLINGS
peanut butter and jelly, ham and mayonnaise, pesto, hummus, sliced avocado

star- and heart-shaped cookie cutters

serves 12

Arrange half the buttered bread slices on a work surface and top with a selection of fillings. Put the remaining bread slices on top and cut out shaped sandwiches with the star and heart cutters.

THE MENU

FOR 12 CHILDREN

Cartwheel Tortilla Wraps

Star and Heart Sandwiches

Cheese Number Puffs

Jam Tarts

Chocolate-Dipped Strawberries

Boys' and Girls' Meringues

Fruit Stars and Hearts

Bedazzled Fairy Cake Mountain

cheese number puffs

You can use other hard cheeses, such as Cheddar, Emmental, or Gruyère, instead of Parmesan.

1 lb. puff pastry dough
1 egg, beaten
4 oz. Parmesan cheese, grated

number-shaped cookie cutters

a baking tray, lightly greased

serves 12

Roll out the dough on a lightly floured surface until very thin. Brush all over with the beaten egg and sprinkle evenly with Parmesan. Using the number cookie cutters, stamp out numbers and transfer them carefully to the baking tray. Cook in a preheated oven at 350°F for 20 minutes until puffed and golden.

85

jam tarts

If you have time, make the dough yourself and get the children to help. They love it and they pick it up so quickly—a little patience goes a long way with dough rolling. If time is short, buy frozen. Make sure you let the tarts cool properly before eating, as jam can get very hot.

1⅓ cups all-purpose flour	12-cup tart pan, buttered
1 stick butter, cut into pieces	4-inch cookie cutter
2 eggs, beaten	
8 oz. fruit jam, about ⅔ cup	serves 12
sugar, for sprinkling	

Put the flour into a mixing bowl and add the butter. Using your fingertips, rub the butter into the flour until the mixture looks like bread crumbs. Gradually add the eggs, using a round-bladed knife to cut the mixture, until it forms a ball. Using your hands, gently knead it in the bowl until the mixture is even. Cover with plastic wrap and chill for 20 minutes.

Transfer the dough to a lightly floured, cool surface and roll out to a large rectangle. Using the cookie cutters, stamp out 12 rounds and use to line the cups in the tart pan. Put 1 teaspoon jam into each tart and sprinkle with a little sugar. Don't use too much jam, or it will bubble over and stick.

Bake the tarts in a preheated oven at 350°F for 20 minutes, then reduce to 300°F and bake for a further 10 minutes until the crusts are golden. If the tarts are a little low on jam, gently heat the remaining jam in a small saucepan. When soft, add a little extra to each tart. Remove from the pan and let cool.

chocolate-dipped strawberries

We all know that children love chocolate—but I find I can balance that by combining it with fruit, such as these beautiful strawberries. Any variety of fruits can be dipped, but the color of strawberries always looks so good.

4 squares (4 oz.) chocolate	parchment paper
4 squares (4 oz.) white chocolate	12 wooden skewers
12 large strawberries	serves 12

Put the chocolate into 2 separate bowls and set the bowls over 2 saucepans of simmering water. When melted, dip the pointed end of each strawberry into one of the chocolates and transfer to the sheet of parchment paper. When set, slide each strawberry onto a skewer and serve.

boys' and girls' meringues

I sometimes call these baby meringues "fairies' wishes." Add a little color to them so they will suit the little pixies at your birthday table!

2 egg whites	a large baking tray, lined with parchment paper
⅓ cup sugar	
red food coloring	
blue food coloring	serves 12

Put the egg whites into a clean bowl and beat until stiff. Add half the sugar and continue beating until stiff and shiny. Remove half the mixture to a second bowl.

Add a drop of red food coloring and half the remaining sugar to the first bowl, beat, and adjust the coloring if you want it stronger. Add a drop of blue food coloring to the second bowl and beat in the remaining sugar.

Using a teaspoon, spoon out onto the prepared baking tray and cook in a preheated oven at 275°F for 2 hours.

THE WORK PLAN

up to a week before

- Make the meringues up to a week in advance and store in a sealed plastic bag (**use a drinking straw to suck out all the excess air**).
- Bake the cakes and let cool.

the day before

- Assemble, frost, and decorate the cake—then hide it!
- Make the cheese number puffs and store in an airtight container.
- Make the tortilla cartwheels, wrap in plastic wrap, and chill.
- Bake the jam tarts and store in an airtight container.

on the day

- Make the sandwiches (except avocado), wrap, and chill.
- Dip the strawberries in chocolate and put onto skewers.

just before serving

- Stamp out the fruit shapes.
- Slice the tortilla cartwheels.
- Make the avocado sandwiches, if using.
- Unwrap and set out the food.

fruit stars and hearts

favorite fruits such as melon, pineapple, kiwifruit, mango, or banana

orange or lemon juice, for brushing

small shaped cutters

serves 12

Cut the fruit into 1/2-inch thick slices. Use the cutters to stamp out shapes. If using apple, pear, or banana, brush them with the juice to prevent them from turning brown.

bedazzled fairy cake mountain

This is a very simple way to make this magic mountain cake—it is just a stack of four cakes in decreasing sizes, all sandwiched together, frosted, and topped with favorite candies or chocolate curls. Instead of candles, try using sparklers or call it a "mud mountain" and cover with chocolate and dark green candies.

6¾ sticks butter

3¾ cups sugar

12 eggs

4½ cups self-rising flour

3 nonstick cake pans, 6, 8, and 10 inches diameter, buttered, plus one paper muffin liner

1 muffin tin or tartlet pan

serves 12

Make the cakes in 2 batches. Put 3 sticks of the butter and 1½ cups of the sugar into a bowl and cream together until light and fluffy. Add 5 of the eggs and beat until well mixed, then add 2 cups of the flour and fold in until smooth. If it seems a little stiff, add a drop of milk.

Transfer to the largest cake pan and bake in a preheated oven at 350°F for about 30–40 minutes until golden, springy in the center, and just coming away from the edges of the pan.

Remove from the oven and let cool for 5 minutes, then remove from the pan and put onto a wire rack to cool.

Mix the remaining ingredients as before, filling the smaller 2 cake pans and the muffin liner. Put the liner into a muffin tin or empty tartlet pan to help keep its shape. Put all 3 cakes into the preheated oven and bake for 25 minutes, checking as before to see if the cakes are cooked. Let cool completely before frosting.

BUTTER FROSTING

2½ sticks softened butter, cut into small pieces

3 cups confectioners' sugar

Put the butter and confectioners' sugar into a bowl, add 2 tablespoons hot water, and beat until soft and creamy.

Put the largest cooled cake onto a wire rack and spread with butter frosting. Put the middle-sized cake on top and spread with butter frosting. Top with the next cake and spread just the middle with butter frosting. Peel the muffin paper away from the smallest cake and put it on top.

TOP FROSTING

Either pick a color and buy candies that are all that color, or have a mishmash of colors to create a jewel-encrusted cake. Choose very small candies, such as jelly beans, M&Ms®, chocolate shapes, tiny silver and gold drops, and licorice bootlaces.

5 cups confectioners' sugar

a big bag of candies

food coloring or unsweetened cocoa powder

grated chocolate

Put the confectioners' sugar into a bowl. If using cocoa powder, mix 3 tablespoons with hot water, add to the confectioners' sugar, and mix. Otherwise just add coloring. Add water a little at a time and stir until smooth and blended. It should be thin enough to run down the cake, but still thick enough to cover it evenly. Pour over the cake, letting it cascade down and cover all of the cake.

While the frosting is still wet, add the candies, sticking them all over the surface, or grate chocolate over the cake. Hide the cake and let set until needed for the lucky birthday child.

the scene

Girls can talk forever, and with this female-only gathering in the relaxed atmosphere of your own home, you can gossip away the afternoon without interruptions. Bliss!

the style

Make the setting indulgent to all things female. Surround yourself with the things you love—flowery tablecloth, plenty of flowers on the table, pretty glasses and cups, an elegant menu. Hide all the clocks so that time ticks by with no one noticing!

girls' reunion lunch

THE WORK PLAN

the day before

- Make the artichoke hummus, cover, and chill.
- Mix the nuts and spices ready for cooking, cover, and store at room temperature.
- Make the dough for the onion tart.
- Freeze the chocolate for the cakes.

on the day

- Bake the pie crust for the tart and cook the onions.
- Prepare the salmon and wrap in prosciutto.
- Slice the zucchini, zest and juice the lemons.
- Assemble and cook the onion tart and make the salsa.
- Cook the nuts and toast the ciabatta.

just before serving

- Make and bake the cakes.
- Cook the salmon.
- Cook the pasta and zucchini ribbons.

THE MENU
FOR 4 PEOPLE

Spiced Nuts

Artichoke Hummus with Ciabatta

Onion Tart

Tomato Salsa

Roasted Salmon Wrapped in Prosciutto

Tossed Zucchini Ribbons and Pasta

Marbled Chocolate Cakes

TO DRINK

Champagne, Chardonnay, Rosé

artichoke hummus with ciabatta

You can make this dip the night before: just remember to remove it from the refrigerator a while before serving so the flavors can warm up. Instead of ciabatta bread, you can serve the hummus with cheese straws, grissini, pita, or other bread for dipping or spreading.

10 oz. artichoke hearts preserved in olive oil, drained

4 oz. drained, canned pinto beans or chickpeas, about ½ cup

sea salt and freshly ground black pepper

ciabatta bread, toasted, to serve

serves 4

Put the artichokes and beans into a food processor and blend until smooth. Transfer to a bowl, add salt and pepper to taste, and serve with the toasted ciabatta.

spiced nuts

Take care that you let these cool before eating—the high oil content and density means they retain heat for longer than you might think.

1 teaspoon cumin seeds	1/3 cup brazil nuts, about 3 oz.
1 teaspoon fennel seeds	1/3 cup almonds, about 3 oz.
1 teaspoon paprika	1/3 cup peanuts, about 3 oz.
1 teaspoon flaked sea salt	1/3 cup shelled pistachios, about 3 oz.
2 tablespoons olive oil	*2 baking trays*
1/3 cup cashews, about 3 oz.	*serves* 4

Crush the cumin and fennel seeds coarsely with a mortar and pestle. Transfer to a bowl and add the paprika, salt, and oil. Mix well, then add all the nuts and mix again to coat. Spread in an even layer on 2 baking trays and roast in a preheated oven at 350°F for 10 minutes. Remove from the oven and turn with a spoon so they cook evenly. Return them to the oven and roast for a further 10 minutes. Remove and set aside to cool.

onion tart

Every good cook should be able to make a savory tart, and this has to be one of the most delicious and popular. As it bakes, it fills your home with gorgeous baking aromas—your girlfriends will be impressed.

Sift the flour into a bowl and add the butter. Using your fingertips, rub the butter into the flour until the mixture looks like fine bread crumbs. Add the beaten eggs and, using a round-bladed knife, cut through the mixture until it forms a ball. Knead lightly in the bowl with floured hands until evenly mixed, then cover and chill for 20 minutes.

Roll out the dough on a lightly floured surface to a circle at least 2 inches bigger in diameter than the base of the tart pan. Drape the dough over the rolling pin, carefully lift it up, and lay it over the top of the pan. Gently press the dough into the pan, making sure there are no air pockets, then use a sharp knife to trim off the excess dough. Chill for 20 minutes.

To make the filling, melt the butter and oil in a saucepan, add the onions, and cook over low heat for 30 minutes until soft and translucent, making sure they don't brown.

Line the pie crust dough with parchment paper and baking beans or rice and bake in a preheated oven at 400°F for 20 minutes. Remove the baking beans or rice and parchment, reduce to 325°F and cook for a further 15 minutes until the crust is set and lightly golden.

Put the eggs and cream into a large bowl and beat until mixed. Add the onions with salt and pepper to taste. Pour into the pie crust and bake in the oven for 25 minutes until set and golden. Serve warm or cold with tomato salsa.

PASTRY DOUGH

1 2/3 cups all-purpose flour, plus extra for dusting

1 3/4 sticks cold butter, cut into small pieces

2 eggs, beaten

FILLING

6 tablespoons butter

2 tablespoons olive oil

1 lb. onions, finely sliced

2 eggs

1/2 cup light cream

sea salt and freshly ground black pepper

a tart pan, 8 inches diameter

parchment paper and baking beans or uncooked rice

serves 4

tomato salsa

4 tomatoes

3 scallions, chopped

freshly squeezed juice of 1 lemon

a bunch of fresh flat-leaf parsley, chopped

sea salt and freshly ground black pepper

serves 4

Cut a cross in the top of each tomato and put into a bowl. Cover with boiling water and leave for 30 seconds, then drain and peel. Cut each tomato into quarters, remove the core and seeds, and chop the flesh. Put into a bowl and add the remaining ingredients. Mix and set aside for 2 hours. Serve with the tart.

When cooking for the girls, keep it light and fresh—except for dessert, when chocolate is a must!

roasted salmon wrapped in prosciutto

What makes this dish such a joy is that you will have no last-minute dramas with the fish falling to pieces, because the prosciutto not only adds flavor and crispness, it also packages up the salmon and makes it easier to handle. Other fish such as trout, cod, halibut, or monkfish are also good.

4 thin slices Fontina cheese, rind removed

4 salmon fillets, 8 oz. each, skinned

4 bay leaves

8 thin slices prosciutto

sea salt and freshly ground black pepper

a baking tray, lightly oiled

serves 4

Trim the Fontina slices to fit on top of the salmon fillets. Put a bay leaf on each fillet, then a slice of the Fontina. Wrap 2 slices of prosciutto around each piece of salmon, so that it is completely covered.

Transfer to the baking tray and cook in a preheated oven at 400°F for about 10–15 minutes, depending on the thickness of the salmon fillets.

tossed zucchini ribbons and pasta

8 oz. dried pappardelle pasta

8 oz. zucchini, very finely sliced lengthwise

finely grated zest and freshly squeezed juice of 1 unwaxed lemon

2 tablespoons extra virgin olive oil

a bunch of chives, finely chopped

sea salt and freshly ground black pepper

serves 4

Cook the pappardelle in a large saucepan of boiling, salted water until *al dente*, or according to the directions on the package. Add the zucchini slices to the pasta for the final 3 minutes of cooking.

Put the lemon zest and juice into a bowl, add the oil and mix. Add the chives, salt, and pepper.

Drain the pasta and zucchini and return them to the pan. Add the lemon juice mixture and toss well to coat, then serve with the roasted salmon.

marbled chocolate cakes

The trick to these indulgent little charms is to put the chocolate chunks into the freezer before you make them, so they don't burn while the cake batter is cooking. They are best eaten 10 minutes after cooking, while the chocolate is soft and runny, but they can be left to cool and reheated for one minute on High in the microwave. Take care, as chocolate can get extremely hot when microwaved.

4 squares (4 oz.) bittersweet chocolate

4 squares (4 oz.) white chocolate

1¾ sticks butter

¾ cup plus 2 tablespoons firmly packed brown sugar

3 large eggs

2 tablespoons cocoa powder

1 cup plus 2 tablespoons self-rising flour

vanilla ice cream or whipped cream, to serve

a 12-cup muffin pan

8 large paper muffin liners

serves 4

Put the chunks of chocolate into the freezer. Arrange the muffin liners in 8 of the cups in the muffin pan.

Put the butter and sugar into a bowl and, using an electric beater, beat until smooth and creamy. Add the eggs and cocoa powder and beat again until blended. Using a large metal spoon, fold in the flour, then fill the muffin liners to just over half full. Add a chunk of bittersweet and white chocolate to each cake, pushing each one lightly into the mixture.

Cook on the middle shelf of a preheated oven at 350°F for 18–20 minutes. Remove from the oven and let cool in the tray for 5–10 minutes. Peel away the muffin liners and serve warm with generous dollops of vanilla ice cream or whipped cream.

beach banquet

the scene

In my dreams, I have a beautiful house far away from any towns, surrounded by sand, sea, and the odd palm tree. It's good to have dreams—they always make me smile on a rainy day. But I would share this state of bliss with friends, serving the most delicious food and wine, sitting in the sunshine, eating, and laughing in this happy pleasure zone.

the style

A beautiful table on the beach set with simple china and flatware—pure and soothing to the eye. The color comes from the food, natural surroundings, and happy people. Decorate the table with seashells, driftwood, and pebbles from the beach.

summer fresh tomato toasts

These are do-it-yourself, so really couldn't be fresher. The taste relies on the garlic being very fresh and clean in its flavor, and the tomatoes being ripe, in season, and packed with a true tomato flavor. This may seem a little messy but you are eating by the sea, so a little dip could be taken between courses, or have extra napkins on the table.

12 ripe tomatoes

8 slices bread

8 garlic cloves, halved crosswise

extra virgin olive oil, for sprinkling

sea salt and freshly ground black pepper

TO SERVE

16 asparagus spears, cooked and cooled

2 handfuls of arugula

serves 8

Cut a cross in each tomato and put into a bowl. Cover with boiling water and leave for 30 seconds, then drain and peel. Toast the bread and let cool in a toast rack.

Arrange plates of toasted bread, garlic, small jugs or bottles of olive oil, tomatoes, salt, and pepper. Encourage everyone to rub the toast with the garlic, sprinkle with olive oil, rub with tomato halves or top with slices of tomato, then sprinkle with salt and pepper. Serve with the asparagus spears and arugula.

THE WORK PLAN

the day before

- Make the shortbread— bake, cover, and store in a cool place.
- Cook the lobsters, if using fresh ones. Remove the flesh, cover, and chill.
- Cook the potatoes for the lobster salad, cover, and chill.
- Peel the tomatoes for the tomato toasts, wrap, and chill.

on the day

- Make the chile dressing.
- Cook the asparagus for the tomato toasts, let cool, then cover.

just before serving

- Assemble the lobster salad.
- Toast the bread.

THE MENU
SERVES 8

Summer Fresh Tomato Toasts

Lobster Salad with Chile Dressing

Coconut and Passionfruit Shortbread Bake

TO DRINK

Chardonnay, Riesling, Rosé, Marsala

lobster salad with chile dressing

Ready-cooked and halved lobsters are easy to find, and some people may prefer to buy them like this rather than prepare them from scratch. But, if you have time and want to cook them yourself, it's well worth it, because you can guarantee that the lobster will be really fresh. If lobsters are difficult to get, or too expensive, try substituting monkfish, often called "poor man's lobster," or even boneless chicken breasts, tossed in olive oil, then roasted in a hot oven for about 25 minutes. Seed the chiles only if you are fearful of heat: I love it, so I leave them in.

8 small or 4 large lobsters

1½ lb. potatoes, cut into chunks

a bunch of cilantro, coarsely chopped

1 red onion, very finely sliced

sea salt and freshly ground black pepper

leafy salad, to serve

CHILE DRESSING

1 green or red chile, seeded (optional) and chopped

2 inches fresh ginger, peeled and chopped

5 garlic cloves

2 tablespoons white wine vinegar

⅓ cup sugar

serves 8

To make the dressing, put the chile, ginger, and garlic into a saucepan. Add the vinegar and sugar and simmer over low heat, stirring frequently, for 10 minutes, until reduced by half. Add 2 tablespoons water, remove from the heat, and let cool.

If cooking the lobsters live, bring a large saucepan of water to a boil. Plunge the lobsters carefully into a boiling water, cover with a lid, and simmer for 10 minutes per pound. Drain and let cool.

When cool, remove the claws and legs. Using a large, sharp knife, split each body in half lengthwise, holding the lobster with a dish cloth in your other hand to stop it slipping. Crack open the claws and remove the flesh, leaving it in whole pieces. Remove the flesh from the split body halves and cut into thick slices. Reserve the shells.

Cook the potatoes in a saucepan of boiling, salted water for 20 minutes, until tender when pierced with a knife. Drain and let cool. Add the cilantro and chopped lobster to the potatoes, with salt and pepper to taste. Mix lightly, then spoon the mixture into the empty lobster shells, piling it in generously. Spoon over the dressing, sprinkle with the onion slices, and serve with a leafy salad. (If using monkfish or chicken serve from a dish decorated with lettuce leaves.)

SHORTBREAD DOUGH

1 stick butter

½ cup sugar

1 cup all-purpose flour

FILLING

7 passionfruit, halved

3 eggs

⅓ cup sugar

⅔ cup unsweetened shredded coconut

⅓ cup all-purpose flour

⅔ cup coconut milk

1 tablespoon confectioners' sugar, for dusting

plain yogurt and cream, or vanilla ice cream, to serve

a springform cake pan, 8 inches diameter, lightly buttered

serves 8

coconut and passionfruit shortbread bake

I love dishes that you make the day before—not only is there less to do on the day but this one actually improves from resting in a cool pantry, so what could be better? The sweetness of the coconut is balanced by the tartness of the passionfruit, creating an elegant dessert.

To make the dough, put the butter and sugar into a bowl and beat with an electric beater or wooden spoon until creamy. Add the flour and rub it in with your fingertips until the mixture looks like bread crumbs. Transfer to the prepared cake pan and flatten gently with the palm of your hand and fingers, lining the base and sides of the pan. Chill while you make the filling.

Using a teaspoon, scoop the passionfruit pulp into a small bowl. Put the eggs and sugar into a large bowl and beat with an electric beater until creamy and doubled in volume. Add the shredded coconut, flour, coconut milk, and passionfruit. Using a large metal spoon, fold until evenly mixed.

Spoon the mixture into the chilled pie crust and bake in a preheated oven at 350°F for 40 minutes. Remove and let cool for 10 minutes, then remove from the pan to a serving plate. Dust with confectioners' sugar and serve with a mixture of plain yogurt and cream, or with ice cream.

THE MENU
FOR 8 PEOPLE

**Feta and Mushroom
Bread Tarts**

**Spicy-Crust Roasted
Rack of Lamb**

**Mashed Minty Potatoes
and Peas**

Paradise Meringues

TO DRINK

**Gewürztraminer or Riesling
with the Tarts,
Cabernet Sauvignon or Shiraz
(Syrah) with the Lamb,
Sauternes with the
Meringues**

elegant dining

the scene

This is formal, grown-up entertaining—for the boss, work associates, or anyone you'd like to impress. The three-course menu is modern and beautifully elegant.

the style

The perfect occasion to get out that matching tableware. For the newly married couple, there is no other time in life when those wedding presents will be as perfect as this. Decorate the table with a few simple stems and try to keep the look clean and uncluttered.

spicy-crust roasted rack of lamb

3 tablespoons cumin seeds

2 tablespoons coriander seeds

2 teaspoons black peppercorns

4 cloves

4 small dried chiles

2 tablespoons sea salt

grated zest and freshly squeezed juice of 2 unwaxed lemons

1/4 cup olive oil

3 racks of lamb, 6 chops each

3/4 cup red wine

serves 8

Heat a dry skillet and add the cumin and coriander seeds, peppercorns, cloves, and chiles. Cook for 1 minute, stirring frequently. Crush coarsely with a mortar and pestle. Transfer to a bowl and stir in the salt, lemon zest and juice, and oil.

Put the racks of lamb into a large roasting pan. Rub the mixture into the lamb, smearing well all over. Cover and chill overnight.

Cook the lamb in a preheated oven at 400°F for 20 minutes then reduce to 350°F. Cook for a further 20 minutes for rare lamb, 25 minutes for medium, and 35 minutes for well done. Remove from the oven, transfer to a carving board, and let rest for 5 minutes in a warm place.

Meanwhile, add the wine and 3/4 cup water to the roasting pan and set it on top of the stove over high heat. Stir to scrape up all the roasted bits on the bottom, and boil until reduced by half.

Cut the lamb into separate chops and arrange on top of the mashed minty potatoes and peas. Spoon a little sauce over the top and serve.

feta and mushroom bread tarts

This may be a formal meal, but that doesn't mean that it has to be complicated—this is a simple recipe with delicious flavors.

2 garlic cloves, crushed

1/4 cup olive oil, plus extra for sprinkling

8 slices white crusty bread

8 portobello mushrooms, stalks removed

4 large tomatoes, quartered and seeded

8 oz. feta cheese, about 1 cup, crumbled

sea salt and freshly ground black pepper

basil or sage, chopped, to serve

serves 8

Put the garlic into a small bowl, add the olive oil, and mix. Smear or brush over both sides of the bread and transfer to a roasting pan. Put a mushroom on each slice of bread. Put 2 tomato quarters on each mushroom and sprinkle with the crumbled feta.

Sprinkle with olive oil, salt, and pepper, then cook in a preheated oven at 350°F for 25 minutes until the bread is golden. Top with your chosen herb and serve hot or warm.

mashed minty potatoes and peas

This simple combination creates a two-in-one vegetable dish, making life in the kitchen a little easier. The mashed potato mixture can be prepared in advance, but don't add the mint until just before serving or it will lose its vibrant, fresh look.

3 lb. boiling potatoes, cut into equal pieces

4 tablespoons butter

1 egg, beaten

½ cup cup milk

10 oz. frozen baby peas, 2 cups

a bunch of mint, chopped

sea salt and freshly ground black pepper

serves 8

Cook the potatoes in a large saucepan of boiling, salted water for about 20 minutes, or until tender when pierced with a knife. Drain well and return them to the pan. Shake the pan a few times, then put over low heat for 2 minutes to steam off any excess moisture.

Add the butter, egg, milk, salt, and pepper. Stir briefly, then remove from the heat and crush the potatoes briefly with the back of a wooden spoon. Keep the potatoes warm while you cook the peas.

Bring a saucepan of salted water to a boil, add the peas, and cook for 2 minutes. Drain, add to the potatoes, then add the mint. Mix gently, crushing the peas lightly into the potato, but keeping some whole.

THE WORK PLAN

the day before

- Make the meringues (or up to a week in advance) and store in an airtight container.
- Prepare the spicy crust, rub it into the lamb, cover, and chill.

on the day

- Peel the potatoes and cover with cold water.
- Make the berry cream and assemble the meringues up to 2 hours in advance. Chill.
- Brush the bread for the mushroom tarts with garlic and oil. Top with the remaining ingredients and put onto the baking tray, ready to cook.

just before serving

- Roast the lamb.
- Cook the potatoes and peas. Put into a bowl and keep them warm.
- Remove the lamb from the oven and keep it warm.
- Cook the feta and mushroom tarts and make the sauce for the lamb.
- Carve the lamb, mix the peas and potatoes.

paradise meringues

These can be made up to a week in advance and then stored in an airtight plastic bag: use a drinking straw to suck out all the excess air, tie up well and store in a cool, dry place.

Put both sugars into a bowl and mix. Put the egg whites into a large, clean bowl and beat until stiff. Add half the sugar mixture and beat again until shiny and stiff. Add the remaining sugar and beat again briefly. Put tablespoons of the mixture onto the prepared baking tray, leaving space between each to let them spread as they cook. Cook in a preheated oven at 225°F for 90 minutes until dry and hard. Remove and let cool.

Put the cream into a bowl and whip until just stiff. Add half the berries and mix briefly to create a marbled effect. Sandwich the meringues together with the berry cream and transfer to individual plates or one serving plate. Sprinkle the remaining berries over the plate, cover, and chill for up to 2 hours before serving.

1/2 cup sugar

1/2 cup firmly packed light brown sugar

4 egg whites

1 1/4 cups heavy cream

1 lb. mixed berries, such as raspberries, strawberries, blueberries, or blackberries

a baking tray, lined with parchment paper

serves 8

after the main event

the scene

If you have a big family celebration with a tent, why not make full use of it the following day for a more relaxed, intimate party. It gives everyone the opportunity to discuss the previous day's events, and the menu is completely cook-ahead, so there isn't much to do on the day.

the style

Tents have a summery feel, with garden furniture and soft pillows and all the flowers still looking their best. Put all the food out on a table and get everyone to help themselves—this is a family and close friends affair, so a bit of informality will be very welcome.

THE MENU

FOR 8 PEOPLE

Osso Buco with Gremolata

Garlic Sautéed Green Beans

Creamy Mashed Potatoes

Coffee and Nut Layer Meringue

Poached Pears and Peaches in Spiced Wine

TO DRINK

Pinot Noir with the Osso Buco, Sauternes with the Desserts

THE WORK PLAN

the day before

- Make the meringues up to a week in advance and store in a sealed plastic bag (use a drinking straw to suck out all the excess air).
- Make the osso buco up to 3 days in advance, cover, and chill.
- Poach the peaches and pears up to 2 days in advance, cover, and chill.

on the day

- Assemble the coffee and nut meringue layer up to 2 hours in advance. Store at room temperature.

just before serving

- Put the pears into a serving dish.
- Reheat the osso buco.
- Peel and cook the potatoes.
- Prepare the beans and garlic.
- Make the gremolata, then cook the beans and mash the potatoes.

osso buco with gremolata

This dish improves when reheated—
it makes a richer, silkier sauce. For
the last 1½ hours of cooking, you can
put this into the oven at 350°F instead
of on top of the stove—but make sure
the casserole is flameproof. Gremolata
is the traditional accompaniment for
osso buco, but it is also lovely with
fish, grills, and white meat roasts.
Make at the last minute, to preserve
its herby zing.

OSSO BUCO

8 veal shank cross cuts
with the marrow bone,
10 oz. each

¼ cup all-purpose flour

¼ cup olive oil

3 garlic cloves, chopped

2 onions, chopped

4 celery stalks, chopped

1 tablespoon tomato
purée

2 cans chopped tomatoes,
15 oz. each, about 4 cups

1 cup dry white wine

1¼ cups vegetable stock

sea salt and freshly
ground black pepper

GREMOLATA

finely grated zest of
3 unwaxed lemons

3 garlic cloves, finely
chopped

a large bunch of fresh
flat-leaf parsley, finely
chopped

serves 8

Dust the veal shanks with
flour. Heat the oil in a large
saucepan, add the veal, and
sauté over medium-low
heat for a few minutes, until
brown all over. Remove
from the pan and set aside.

Add a little more oil to the
pan if needed, heat, and
add the garlic, onions, and
celery. Cook for 5 minutes
until soft but not browned.
Add the tomato purée and
tomatoes, mix well, and add
the wine, stock, salt, and
pepper. Return the meat
to the pan and gently bring
to a boil. Cover with a lid
and simmer gently for
1½ hours, adding a little
more stock or wine from
time to time if needed.
Let cool, cover, and chill.

When ready to serve, put
the osso buco into a
preheated oven at 350°F
until simmering, then
continue cooking for
15 minutes or until heated
right through.

Meanwhile, to make the
gremolata, put the lemon
zest, garlic, and parsley into
a bowl and stir well.

Remove the osso buco
from the oven and serve
topped with gremolata.

garlic sautéed green beans

It may seem odd not to cook the beans in a pan of water, but with this method the beans take on a wonderful buttery, garlic flavor, while keeping their crunchy texture.

2 garlic cloves, crushed and finely chopped

2 tablespoons butter

2 tablespoons olive oil

8 oz. runner beans, trimmed and cut into 3 pieces each

8 oz. green beans, trimmed

8 oz. sugar snap peas, trimmed

freshly ground black pepper

serves 8

Put the garlic, butter, and oil into a large saucepan and heat gently. When hot, add all the beans and sugar snap peas and cook, stirring frequently, for 5 minutes until tender but still slightly crisp. Sprinkle with plenty of black pepper and serve.

creamy mashed potatoes

All sorts of different and wonderful flavors can be added to mashed potatoes. However, since the osso buco has such richly intense flavor, this time keep the potatoes plain. If serving with simpler flavors, such as grilled fish or lamb chops, try adding chopped herbs, cheese such as goat, blue, or mascarpone, saffron threads (just steep in a little hot water before adding), wholegrain mustard, or scallions.

3 lb. potatoes, cut into equal pieces

4 tablespoons butter

¼ cup olive oil

½ cup cream or milk

2 heaped teaspoons dry mustard powder, mixed to a paste with water

sea salt and freshly ground black pepper

serves 8

Cook the potatoes in a saucepan of boiling, salted water for 20 minutes, until tender when pierced with a knife. Drain well and return to the pan. Set over low heat for 2 minutes to steam off the excess moisture. Remove from the heat and mash thoroughly. Add the butter, oil, cream or milk, mustard, salt, and pepper. Mix well, or blend until smooth and creamy with an electric beater.

coffee and nut layer meringue

To be sure of even cooking, you may need to switch the meringues from shelf to shelf at various stages during cooking.

6 egg whites

1¾ cups sugar

3 oz. chopped mixed nuts, about ⅔ cup

2¾ cups heavy cream

2 tablespoons confectioners' sugar, plus extra for dusting

1 tablespoon instant coffee

3 oz. chopped walnuts, about ⅔ cup

3 baking trays, lined with parchment paper

serves 8

Put a dinner plate upside down on each lined baking tray and draw around it with a dark-colored pen. Turn the paper over and use the circles as your guideline.

Put the egg whites into a large, clean bowl and beat until stiff and fluffy. Add half the sugar and beat again until smooth and shiny. Add the remaining sugar and nuts and beat briefly. Divide the mixture between the 3 drawn circles on the baking trays. Spread out with the back of a spoon to fill the circles. Bake in a preheated oven at 275°F for 1 hour, until firm on the outside but still soft in the middle.

Put the cream into a bowl and beat until soft. Put the confectioners' sugar and coffee into a cup and add just enough boiling water to dissolve the coffee. Add the coffee and walnuts to the cream and mix carefully until evenly blended.

To assemble, put a spoonful of cream onto a large serving plate: this will help secure the meringue. Put one of the meringue layers on top and spread with half the cream mixture. Add another meringue layer and spread with the remaining cream mixture. Top with the final meringue layer and dust with confectioners' sugar. Chill for up to 2 hours before serving.

poached pears and peaches in spiced wine

These can be served on their own or with the coffee and nut layer meringue. Buy ripe and juicy peaches—the pits are easier to remove.

8 pears, peeled with stalk still attached

1 bottle red wine, 750 ml

1 star anise

2 cardamom pods

4 cloves

1 unwaxed lemon, sliced

½ cup sugar

4 peaches, halved crosswise and pitted

cream or mascarpone, to serve

serves 8

Put the pears into a saucepan and add the wine, star anise, cardamom pods, cloves, lemon slices, and sugar. Slowly bring to a boil, then simmer for 15 minutes. Remove from the heat and add the peach halves. Set aside for 1 hour to infuse. Serve warm or cold with the coffee and nut layer meringue, or with cream or mascarpone.

THE WORK PLAN

the day before

- Marinate the chicken, cover, and chill.
- Roast the rice for the duck salad. Roast the duck, make the dressing, cover, and chill.

on the day

- Make the syrupy banana rice cake. (Reheat in the pan briefly before turning it out onto a plate, to stop it sticking.)
- Cook the chicken.
- Make the laksa, but don't add the scallions.

just before serving

- Assemble the duck salad.
- Make the fruit salad.

THE MENU
FOR 8 PEOPLE

Seafood Laksa

Thai-Style Duck Salad

Korean Chicken

Exotic Fruit Salad

Syrupy Banana Rice Cake

TO DRINK

Lager, Riesling, Pinot Noir

the scene

This sort of feast is a real treat for the taste buds, and with all the ingredients readily available, you can recreate that Asian restaurant in your own home.

the style

Let your imagination run wild and indulge in all those beautiful, dramatic eastern looks—a low table, a colorful runner down the middle, chopsticks, and exotic flowers.

eastern feast

seafood laksa

This is a meal in itself and always hugely popular.

8 oz. rice noodles

2 tablespoons peanut oil

1 onion, sliced

2 garlic cloves, chopped

2 inches fresh ginger, peeled and chopped

1 stalk of lemongrass, bruised and chopped

1 red chile, finely sliced

1½ lb. uncooked jumbo shrimp, peeled

½ teaspoon ground turmeric

½ teaspoon ground coriander

2 cups coconut milk

3 cups fish or vegetable stock

1 tablespoon fish sauce

freshly squeezed juice of 1 lime

8 oz. fresh bean sprouts, 2 cups

a bunch of scallions, sliced

serves 8

Put the noodles into a bowl and cover with boiling water. Let soak until soft, about 10 minutes, or according to the directions on the package, then drain.

Heat the oil in a large saucepan and add the onion, garlic, ginger, lemongrass, chile, and shrimp. Cook over medium heat for 5 minutes, stirring frequently. Add the turmeric and coriander and cook for a further 2 minutes. Add the coconut milk, stock, fish sauce, lime juice, bean sprouts, noodles, and scallions. Mix well and bring to a very gentle simmer for about 2 minutes, then serve.

Thai-style duck salad

This duck salad may seem a bit long and complicated, but every time I serve it, everyone has been fascinated and wants to know how I made it. So, if you have inquisitive taste buds, I urge you to try this dish. Shrimp, beef, or pork can be used instead of the duck.

¾ cup jasmine rice

4 duck legs

1 tablespoon fish sauce

2 inches fresh ginger, peeled and chopped

2 inches galangal or extra fresh ginger, peeled and chopped

3 stalks of lemongrass, finely sliced

6 kaffir lime leaves

½ cup coconut milk

3 green mangoes, peeled and cut into matchsticks

4 oz. Chinese yard-long beans, finely sliced

2 chiles, finely chopped

4 oz. Chinese cabbage or iceberg lettuce, shredded

a bunch of basil, preferably Thai basil

a bunch of cilantro, chopped

⅓ cup cashews, chopped, to serve

DRESSING

1 bird's eye chile, seeded and finely chopped

1 tablespoon fish sauce

freshly squeezed juice of 3 limes

1 teaspoon tamarind paste

serves 8

Put the rice into a bowl, cover with cold water, and soak for 5 minutes. Drain, then sprinkle evenly over a baking tray. Cook in a preheated oven at 400°F for 30 minutes until golden and starting to pop. Crush coarsely with a mortar and pestle. Keep the oven at the same temperature.

Put the duck legs into a roasting pan and add the fish sauce, ginger, galangal, if using, lemongrass, 4 of the kaffir lime leaves, and the coconut milk. Transfer to the preheated oven and roast for 30 minutes, then reduce to 350°F and cook for a further 40 minutes, until the skin is golden and crisp. Remove from the oven and let cool. When cool, shred the duck into bite-size pieces, discarding the bones, and put into a large bowl with all the bits and juices from the roasting pan.

Add the mango, yard-long beans, chiles, and cabbage or lettuce to the bowl. Finely shred the remaining 2 lime leaves and add to the bowl. Just before serving, add the basil leaves, cilantro, and crushed rice and mix well.

To make the dressing, put the chile, fish sauce, lime juice, and tamarind paste into a small bowl or measuring cup. Stir well, then just before serving, pour over the salad, and toss gently. Sprinkle with chopped cashews and serve.

korean chicken

Remove and discard any excess fat from the chicken pieces and drain off the oil while cooking.

4 lb. chicken pieces, trimmed

¼ cup sesame oil

½ cup light soy sauce

4 garlic cloves, very finely chopped

1 teaspoon chile powder

5 scallions, very finely chopped

freshly ground black pepper

TO SERVE

1 lb. dried egg noodles

1 teaspoon black sesame seeds (optional)

serves 8

Put the chicken into an ovenproof dish, add the sesame oil, soy sauce, garlic, chile powder, scallions, and black pepper to taste. Mix well, cover, and chill overnight.

Uncover the chicken and transfer to a preheated oven at 350°F for 30 minutes. Reduce to 275°F and cook for a further 40 minutes. Meanwhile, cook the noodles according to the directions on the package. Drain, then serve the chicken and noodles, sprinkled with the sesame seeds, if using.

exotic fruit salad

Not an apple or orange in sight in this exotic fruit salad. I like it to be full of fruit from the tropics, chosen according to cost and what's in season. Include no more than four varieties, so the individual flavors will be strong and sharp.

choose from sweet pineapple, mango, papaya, bananas, lychee, fresh coconut, watermelon, melon, pomegranate, passionfruit, or persimmon

freshly squeezed juice of 4 limes

serves 8

Prepare the chosen fruits, arrange on a serving dish, then squeeze the juice of 4 limes over the top.

syrupy banana rice cake

If Southeast Asia were to have a version of tarte Tatin, this would be it—if you like sticky hot bananas and rice pudding, this was invented for you.

1/3 cup firmly packed brown sugar

2 tablespoons butter

6 bananas, sliced

1 cup white rice, cooked, drained and cooled

2 eggs, beaten

1/2 teaspoon vanilla extract

1/2 teaspoon freshly grated nutmeg

1/4 cup sugar

2/3 cup self-rising flour

serves 8

Put the brown sugar and butter into an ovenproof skillet and put over medium-high heat. When melted and bubbling, add the bananas, in layers. Put the cooked rice, egg, vanilla extract, and nutmeg into a bowl and mix. Add the sugar and flour and stir until smooth. Spoon the mixture over the bananas, spreading it evenly with the back of a spoon. Transfer the pan to a preheated oven and bake at 350°F for 35 minutes until set and golden. Let cool for 5 minutes, then turn out, banana side up, onto a large plate. Serve warm, at room temperature, or cold.

teenage party

the scene

Friends are of the utmost importance when you are a teenager. Parties are an essential part of this exciting stage of life: the music, the clothes, the dancing—and of course the food as well.

the style

Set out the food and accessories on a table, for people to help themselves. Have lots of napkins, drinking straws, glasses, and extra plates—the food is so good they will keep coming back for more.

THE MENU

FOR 24 PEOPLE

Chicken Sticks with Sweet Chile

Herby Hamburgers

Potato Skins with Green Dip

Vegetarian Mexican Rolls

Chocolate Chip Cookie Ice Cream Cakes

DRINKS

Apple and Mint Fizz, Ginger Beer

apple and mint fizz

There is something satisfying and traditional about making your own drinks. This one is simple, refreshing and also popular on hot summer days.

a large bunch of mint

2 quarts apple juice

1 quart sparkling water

ice cubes, to serve

makes about 3 quarts

Reserve some of the mint leaves for serving and put the remainder into a heat-proof pitcher. Add 1 1/4 cups boiling water, let cool, then chill.

Transfer to a large container and add the apple juice, sparkling water, and ice cubes. Chop the reserved mint leaves, sprinkle over the top, and serve.

ginger beer

This seems a large quantity of ginger beer but it's so easy to make and it does store well. Take care that the bottle tops are secure, as they can sometimes pop off.

3 unwaxed lemons

3 1/4 cups sugar

8 oz. fresh ginger, peeled and sliced

2 teaspoons cream of tartar

1 tablespoon brewer's yeast

makes about 6 quarts

Cut the yellow zest off the lemons in strips, then remove and discard the white pith. Finely slice the lemon flesh, removing all the pits. Put the lemon flesh and zest into a large bowl. Add the sugar, ginger, cream of tartar, and about 6 quarts boiling water and let stand until tepid.

Sprinkle in the yeast and stir. Cover with plastic wrap and let stand in a warm place for 24 hours. Using a large metal spoon, skim off the yeast, then carefully pour the mixture through a strainer, leaving behind any sediment. Pour into bottles with secure tops and leave for 2 days before drinking. Serve chilled with ice.

THE WORK PLAN

the day before

- Make the ginger beer (up to a week in advance).
- Marinate the chicken, cover, and chill.
- Make and shape the burgers, cover, and chill.
- Bake the potatoes, scoop out the middles, and cut the skins into wedges.

on the day

- Make the cookies, let cool, and sandwich together with ice cream. Freeze.
- Make the dip for the potato skins, then cook the skins up to the point of adding cheese.
- Prepare the vegetables for the burgers.
- Cook the chicken sticks.
- Make the vegetarian rolls.

just before serving

- Cook the burgers to order.
- Sprinkle the potato skins with cheese and finish cooking.
- Make the apple and mint fizz.

chicken sticks with sweet chile

Chicken sticks are always very popular, so it's worth making extra. You can use boneless chicken thighs, but always remove any excess fat. They may also need to cook for a little longer, as the meat is denser.

12 boneless, skinless chicken breasts, cut into 10 cubes each

2 tablespoons honey

1¾ cups chile sauce

olive oil, for brushing

24 bamboo satay sticks, soaked in water for about 30 minutes

serves 24

Put the chicken, honey and chile sauce into a bowl and mix well. Cover and chill overnight. When ready to cook, thread the chicken cubes onto the soaked satay sticks. Heat the broiler to medium-high and brush the rack of the broiler pan with oil.

Add the chicken sticks to the rack and cook, in batches if necessary, turning frequently, for 25 minutes, or until the chicken is cooked through. Repeat until all the chicken sticks are cooked, then serve hot or cold.

herby hamburgers

The best way to get a good, even mixture is with your hands. Don't be tempted to use ordinary burger buns—a good, crusty roll makes all the difference.

2¹/₂ lb. best-quality ground beef

8 shallots, finely chopped

5 garlic cloves, chopped

a bunch of flat-leaf parsley, chopped

a bunch of chives, chopped

a bunch of tarragon, chopped

2 teaspoons sea salt

2 teaspoons freshly ground black pepper

3 tablespoons Worcestershire sauce

1 teaspoon Tabasco sauce

TO SERVE

crusty rolls or ciabatta rolls

beef tomatoes, sliced

arugula or watercress

red onions, finely sliced

scallions

mustard, mayonnaise, tomato ketchup

wax paper

serves 24

Put all the burger ingredients into a large bowl and, using your hands, mix until evenly blended. Divide the mixture into 24 balls and pat into hamburger shapes. Arrange in layers on a large plate with squares of wax paper between each burger. Cover and chill until needed.

Cook at a high heat either on a preheated outdoor grill or in a skillet, preferably nonstick, for 3 minutes on each side for medium and 5 minutes each side for well done.

Set out all the burger ingredients and let people assemble their own.

potato skins with green dip

The cheese can be either melted and soft or crisp and crunchy—keep checking and remove at the right moment. Save the potato middles for making mashed potatoes.

12 large baking potatoes

¾ cup olive oil

14 oz. sharp Cheddar cheese, grated, about 4 cups

GREEN DIP

1¾ cups sour cream

2 bunches of chives, chopped

2 bunches of scallions, chopped

a bunch of flat-leaf parsley, chopped

sea salt and freshly ground black pepper

a baking tray, lightly oiled

serves 24

Using a small, sharp knife, pierce each potato right through the middle. Bake in a preheated oven at 350°F for 1 hour 10 minutes until cooked through. Remove and set aside until cool enough to handle. Cut each potato in half lengthwise and, using a spoon, scoop out the soft potato middles, leaving a thin layer lining the skin. Cut each skin half into 4 wedges, then cover and chill until needed.

Brush oil over the potato skins and arrange in a single layer on the prepared baking tray. Bake at the top of a preheated oven at 425°F for 30 minutes until golden, moving the potatoes around occasionally so they cook evenly. Remove from the oven and reduce the heat to 400°F. Sprinkle with cheese and return to the oven for 5–10 minutes, until the cheese is melted or crunchy, checking after 5 minutes if you want it melted.

To make the dip, put the sour cream, chives, scallions, and parsley into a bowl. Add salt and pepper to taste and mix well. Serve with the potato skins for dipping.

vegetarian mexican rolls

These are best made to order or at the last moment, otherwise the avocado will discolor. You could encourage everyone to roll their own by setting out all the fillings in bowls and leaving the avocados whole, for everyone to slice as needed.

12 soft large flour tortillas

8 oz. cream cheese, 1 cup

4 carrots, grated

a bunch of cilantro, chopped

a bunch of chives, chopped

a bunch of scallions, chopped

2 chiles, chopped

4 avocados, halved, pitted, peeled, and sliced

freshly squeezed juice of 2 lemons

¼ cup olive oil, plus extra to serve

sea salt and freshly ground black pepper

serves 24

Put each tortilla onto an individual sheet of plastic wrap. Spread with the cream cheese and then sprinkle evenly with the carrot, cilantro, chives, scallions, and chiles. Flatten the topping lightly with a spatula.

Put the avocado slices into a bowl and sprinkle with lemon juice, oil, salt, and pepper. Arrange over the open tortillas. Roll each tortilla into a tight cylinder, using the plastic wrap to help you roll. Twist both ends in opposite directions to make a cigar shape. Chill until needed, then slice in half, with the plastic wrap still on, and serve.

3¹⁄₂ sticks butter

1³⁄₄ cups plus
2 tablespoons
sugar

3 eggs

1 teaspoon vanilla
extract

2¹⁄₂ cups
all-purpose flour

13 squares (13 oz.)
bittersweet
chocolate,
chopped

2¹⁄₂ quarts ice
cream

*2 baking trays,
lined with
parchment paper*

serves 24

chocolate chip cookie ice cream cakes

What a combination! Two of my favorite sweet things sandwiched together. If you really do run out of time and can't make the cookies then by all means buy them, but they will not be as good as my recipe!

Put the butter and sugar into a bowl and beat until light and fluffy. Add the eggs and vanilla and beat well. (The mixture will separate, but this is not a problem.) Add the flour and chocolate and fold until smooth. Working in batches, spoon out 48 portions of the mixture (2 teaspoons each) onto the prepared baking trays, making sure each cookie has enough room to spread (they will triple in size). Bake in the middle of a preheated oven at 350°F for about 15 minutes until lightly golden. Remove from the oven and let cool on the baking trays for 5 minutes. Transfer to a wire cooling rack and let cool completely.

Sandwich 2 cookies together with ice cream, arrange on a tray, cover well with foil, and return to the freezer until needed. Remove 20 minutes before serving so the ice cream can soften a little.

waterside feast

the scene

If I had a house by the sea or a river, I would have a party like this once a week. Just imagine swimming, eating, chatting, eating, dipping, laughing, and eating again—it's such an easy, happy way to socialize, and the variety of dishes breaks up the formality of a three-course meal. It's the sort of gathering that might start at midday and roll on until dusk. The secret with the food is to avoid putting it all out at once and to encourage guests to cook their own.

the style

A little organization is needed with this gathering, but it is very flexible. You really don't want to be scraping plates and washing up—so go on, be brave and pay someone to come and do it for you. Set a really large table with all the abundance of the feast and have the outdoor grill nearby. Use a separate table for drinks and chill your bottles in brightly colored plastic boxes.

THE MENU

FOR 20 PEOPLE

Vodka Watermelon

Sesame-Crusted Marlin with Ginger Dressing

Pork Satay with Spiced Dip

Sweet Glazed Bell Pepper Salad

Mozzarella Baked Tomatoes

Noodle Mountain

Blue and Red Berry Tarts

TO DRINK

Pinot Blanc, Chardonnay

THE WORK PLAN

the day before

- Make the tart shells, store in a cool place.
- Prepare the pork and marinate overnight.
- Prepare the tomatoes, cover, and chill.

on the day

- Make the vodka watermelon and chill.
- Cook the bell peppers and onions.
- Dip the marlin steaks in sesame seeds, cover, and chill until needed.
- Make the ginger dressing.
- Make the spiced dip for the pork.

just before serving

- Assemble the fruit tarts.
- Cook the marlin, pork, and tomatoes.
- Assemble the bell pepper salad.
- Make the noodle mountain.

vodka watermelon

This tastes and looks heavenly, but has the effect of dynamite!
If you can't get seedless watermelon, just use regular and seed it.

1 seedless watermelon, chilled

1 bottle chilled vodka, 750 ml

lime wedges and ice, to serve

serves 20

Cut the melon in half and scoop out all the flesh. Put into a blender and process until smooth. Remove to a large pitcher, add the vodka and let chill for 2 hours before serving. For a less alcoholic version, add sparkling water, or lemonade for those with a sweet tooth. Serve with lime wedges and ice.

sesame-crusted marlin with ginger dressing

Marlin is fantastic for the outdoor grill, as it is firm and doesn't break up when turned. It's a dense fish with an intense flavor, so serve it in small portions. Swordfish also works well.

20 marlin or swordfish steaks, about 4 oz. each

5 egg whites*

1½ lb. toasted sesame seeds

1 tablespoon hot red pepper flakes

GINGER DRESSING

14 oz. fresh ginger, peeled and finely chopped

2¾ cups light soy sauce

2 bunches of scallions, chopped

¼ cup sesame oil

serves 20

Dry the marlin steaks with paper towels. Put the egg whites into a bowl and beat until frothy. Put the sesame seeds and hot red pepper flakes onto a large plate and mix. Dip each marlin steak first into the egg whites, then into the sesame seeds and pepper flakes, until evenly coated on both sides. Cook under a medium-hot broiler or on a preheated outdoor grill for 5 minutes on each side.

To make the dressing, put the ginger, soy sauce, scallions, and sesame oil into a bowl and mix. Spoon the dressing over the marlin and serve.

*Note Use the leftover egg whites from the tart dough.

pork satay with spiced dip

This yogurt dip is fresh and different and, as it's nut-free, it's great if you have any allergy worries. You can also use chicken or beef instead of pork.

4 pork tenderloins, about 14 oz. each, cut into 1½-inch cubes

¼ cup mild curry powder

½ cup ground coriander

13 oz. fresh ginger, peeled and grated

4 garlic cloves, crushed and finely chopped

¼ cup soy sauce

¼ cup canola oil

SPICED DIP

½ cup mild curry powder

2 large bunches of cilantro, chopped

2 cups plain yogurt

20 long metal skewers

serves 20

Put the pork into a bowl and add the curry powder, ground coriander, ginger, garlic, soy sauce, oil, and ⅓ cup water. Mix well, cover, and chill for at least 1 hour, preferably overnight.

Thread the pork onto the skewers and cook under a hot broiler or on a preheated outdoor grill for about 20 minutes, turning frequently, until cooked through.

Put the dip ingredients into a bowl and mix. Serve with the pork.

sweet glazed bell pepper salad

For centuries, Italians have been eating roasted bell peppers and they are truly wonderful. Don't think that there are far too many in this recipe. Not true—I can promise you, it will all disappear!

10 red bell peppers, cut into large chunks and seeded

5 red onions, quartered lengthwise

1/4 cup olive oil

1/3 cup balsamic vinegar

2 tablespoons honey

12 oz. pitted kalamata or other black olives, chopped, about 2 1/2 cups

sea salt and freshly ground black pepper

a sprig of parsley, to serve

serves 20

Put the bell peppers and onions into a large bowl, add the olive oil, and mix to coat. Transfer to 2 large roasting pans and cook in a preheated oven at 350°F for 1 hour, turning the vegetables after 40 minutes so they will cook evenly. Add the vinegar, honey, olives, salt, and pepper, mix well, and set aside to cool. Serve warm or cold, topped with a sprig of parsley.

mozzarella baked tomatoes

If you can find it, use purple basil, which looks even more spectacular than green. This dish really couldn't be easier, and makes a nice change from roasted tomato halves.

20 ripe tomatoes

8 oz. fresh mozzarella cheese, drained and cut into 20 pieces

½ **cup olive oil**

a bunch of basil, torn

sea salt and freshly ground black pepper

a large baking tray, lightly oiled

serves 20

Cut a deep cross, to about half way down, in the top of each tomato and stuff a piece of mozzarella into each. Transfer to the baking tray and sprinkle with salt and pepper. Cook in a preheated oven at 325°F for 25 minutes until the tomatoes are beginning to soften and open up. Sprinkle with oil and basil and serve warm.

I love showing off in the kitchen, so cooking for friends is always great fun. Often I start to organize a small dinner and it ends up with twenty people— I just can't stop gathering everyone together!

noodle mountain

Any vegetarians at your party will be grateful for the wide selection of dishes you have provided, so don't be daunted by this large mountain— they'll love it. Other vegetables can always be added, such as asparagus, baby corn, thin green beans, carrots, mushrooms, or water chestnuts.

12 oz. dried egg noodles

$^1/_3$ cup canola oil

4 garlic cloves, chopped

5 inches fresh ginger, peeled and chopped

4 onions, finely sliced

4 chiles, finely chopped

1 Chinese cabbage, finely shredded

8 oz. bean sprouts, about 2 cups

$^3/_4$ cup soy sauce

freshly squeezed juice of 4 limes

2 bunches of scallions, chopped

14 oz. cashews, chopped, about 2$^1/_2$ cups

serves 20

Cook the noodles according to the directions on the package, drain, and transfer to a bowl of cold water. Reserve.

Heat the oil in a wok and add the garlic, ginger, onions, and chiles. Cook over medium heat for 5 minutes until softened. Add the cabbage and bean sprouts and stir briefly. Drain the noodles well and add to the wok. Toss with 2 large spoons, then add the soy sauce, lime juice, scallions, and cashews. Mix well and serve.

PASTRY DOUGH

4¾ cups all-purpose flour,
plus extra for dusting

¾ cup sugar

4¾ sticks butter

6 egg yolks

FILLING

10 oz. blueberries, about 2 cups

2½ cups confectioners' sugar,
plus extra for dusting

6 cups heavy cream

2 lb. strawberries, hulled and cut into
bite-size pieces

1 lb. raspberries, about 3 cups

10 oz. blackberries, about 2 cups

*3 loose-bottom tart pans, 9 inches
diameter, buttered*

*wax paper and baking beans or
uncooked rice*

serves 20

blue and red berry tarts

Make these mixed fruit tarts and I promise you they will just disappear—no one can resist perfect crumbling crust piled with mixed fruits and served with softly whipped cream. With this quantity of dough, it's easiest to make it in two batches, saving the leftover egg whites for the marlin coating (page 127).

Put half the flour, half the sugar, and half the butter into a food processor and blend until the mixture looks like bread crumbs. Add 3 of the egg yolks and process again until the mixture forms a ball. Remove and repeat with the remaining dough ingredients. Combine, then divide into 3 equal amounts. Wrap separately in plastic wrap and chill for about 20 minutes.

Transfer to a lightly floured surface and roll out each dough portion until just larger than the tart pans. Line each pan with dough, prick the base with a fork, and chill for 20 minutes.

Line the chilled pie crust doughs with wax paper and baking beans or rice. Cook in a preheated oven at 350°F for 20 minutes.

Remove the baking beans and paper, reduce to 325°F, and cook for a further 20 minutes until dry and golden.

Put the blueberries and 1¼ cups confectioners' sugar into a small saucepan. Add ½ cup water and simmer gently for 5 minutes until the berries are soft. Remove from the heat and let cool.

Put the cream into a bowl, add the remaining confectioners' sugar, and whip until soft peaks form. Add the strawberries, mix briefly, then spoon into the cooled pie crusts. Pile the raspberries and blackberries on top. Spoon over the stewed blueberries, remove the tarts from the pans, and serve dusted with confectioners' sugar.

THE MENU

FOR 12 PEOPLE

Chicken Jalfrezi

Chickpea and Vegetable Curry

Crusted Rice Cake

Tomato and Onion Salad

Naan Bread and Pappadams

Caramelized Orange and Pineapple

TO DRINK

**Lager,
Sauvignon Blanc,
Viognier**

party buffet

the scene

The menu is predominantly Indian. It's great for serving to a crowd—the dishes can be made in advance and the flavors will only improve.

the style

Let the interior designer in you show off with lengths of sari fabric, strings of flowers, and dazzling, colorful cloth. If it's an outdoor party, put rugs on the ground and scatter pillows around a low table for a touch of exotic decadence.

THE WORK PLAN

the day before

- Make the chicken jalfrezi, let cool, cover, and chill. (Reheat gently in the oven and add lemon and herbs just before serving.)

on the day

- Soak and prepare the crusted rice cake.
- Slice the oranges and pineapple.
- Make the chickpea and vegetable curry.

just before serving

- Make the tomato and onion salad.
- Make the caramel—if you are making spun sugar, this must be done at the last minute, but if serving as a sauce, it can be made earlier in the day.

1/4 cup canola oil

3 large onions, sliced

3 garlic cloves, chopped

2 inches fresh ginger, peeled and chopped

4 chiles, chopped

2 teaspoons ground turmeric

4 cardamom pods, lightly crushed

4 teaspoons curry powder

2 teaspoons ground coriander

2 teaspoons ground cumin

4 lb. boneless, skinless chicken breasts, cut into chunks

3 cans chopped tomatoes, 15 oz. each, about 6 cups

freshly squeezed juice of 2 limes

freshly squeezed juice of 1 lemon

a large bunch of cilantro, chopped, to serve

sea salt and freshly ground black pepper

serves 12

chicken jalfrezi

This curry can also be made with beef, lamb, shrimp, or fish instead of chicken. If using fish, choose a firm white variety such as swordfish, marlin, monkfish, or kingfish, or whatever your fish seller recommends.

Heat the oil in a large saucepan, add the onion, garlic, ginger, and chiles, and cook until soft, making sure they do not brown or frizzle. Add the turmeric, cardamom, curry powder, ground coriander, and cumin and cook for 2 minutes. Add the chicken, sprinkle with salt and pepper, and stir until coated with the spices. Cook for 5 minutes until the chicken is opaque on the outside. Add the tomatoes, mix well, cover with a lid, and simmer for 30 minutes, stirring from time to time. If making in advance, make up to this point, cool, and chill. Add the lime and lemon juices, simmer for 3 minutes, and serve with the chopped cilantro.

chickpea and vegetable curry

We eat a lot of this curry at home as it's simple to make and usually we have the ingredients to hand. I often call it my end-of-the-week curry when there is not much else in the house. You can change any of the vegetables to suit availability, but I always avoid carrots and peas—they don't seem authentic. As with all curries this can be made in advance and left overnight for the flavors to deepen and intensify.

3 tablespoons canola oil

2 garlic cloves, crushed

2 red onions, chopped

2 inches fresh ginger, peeled and chopped

1 tablespoon curry powder

2 teaspoons ground coriander

1/2 teaspoon fenugreek (optional)

1/2 teaspoon hot red pepper flakes

1 can chopped tomatoes, 15 oz., about 2 cups

1 1/2 lb. potatoes, cut into 1-inch pieces

1 cauliflower, cut into florets

2 cans chickpeas, 15 oz. each, about 4 cups, drained and rinsed

1 lb. spinach, washed, dried, and coarsely chopped

8 oz. okra, washed, dried, and halved lengthwise

serves 12

Heat the oil in a large saucepan, add the garlic, onion, and ginger, and cook over low heat for 10 minutes until softened. Add the curry powder, coriander, fenugreek, if using, and pepper flakes, mix well, and cook for another 4 minutes. Add the tomatoes and 1/2 cup water, then add the potatoes, cauliflower, and chickpeas. Mix well, cover with a lid, and simmer for 15 minutes, stirring frequently. Add the spinach and okra, mix well, and simmer for 5 minutes. You may need to add a little extra water at this final stage. Serve with the chicken jalfrezi, crusted rice cake, tomato and onion salad, naan bread, and pappadams.

crusted rice cake

Rice can be a delicious staple at large gatherings, and this great Persian recipe not only tastes divine but is stunning too. The trick to this dish is to use a good pan with a tight fitting lid, such as Le Creuset. A heavy skillet will also work.

2¹/₂ cups basmati rice

¹/₂ teaspoon saffron threads

1 stick butter

1 cinnamon stick

3 cloves

3 cardamom pods

¹/₃ cup raisins

6 dried apricots, soaked in water for 30 minutes, then chopped

serves 12

Soak the rice in cold water for 1 hour, drain, and rinse under the tap until the water runs clear. Bring a large saucepan of water to a boil, then add the rice. Simmer for 3 minutes, adding the saffron threads after 2 minutes, then drain well.

Melt 6 tablespoons of the butter in a skillet, then add half the drained rice and flatten slightly with the back of a spoon. Remove from the heat. Put the cinnamon stick, cloves, cardamom, raisins, and apricots into a bowl and mix. Spread in a layer on top of the rice. Top with the remaining rice and flatten with the back of a spoon. Cut the remaining butter into small pieces and dot over the rice. Cover the pan with a clean, dry dish cloth and then with a fitted lid. Turn up and secure any excess cloth (or tie the corners together), to stop it catching fire, and put over the lowest heat for about 30 minutes. Remove from the heat and let stand for 15 minutes with the lid on, then turn out the rice cake onto a large plate. Serve hot, at room temperature, or cold.

tomato and onion salad

Be generous with the parsley and cilantro—they act as palate fresheners after a spicy curry.

6 beef tomatoes

2 red onions, finely sliced

1 white onion, chopped

a bunch of scallions, sliced

a bunch of flat-leaf parsley, chopped

a bunch of cilantro, chopped

¹/₄ cup olive oil

1 tablespoon white wine vinegar

1 tablespoon crushed mustard seeds

sea salt and freshly ground black pepper

serves 12

Cut a cross in the top of each tomato and put them into a large bowl. Cover with boiling water, leave for 30 seconds, then drain and peel. Chop the tomatoes coarsely and put into a large bowl. Add all the onion and scallions, then add the parsley, cilantro, oil, vinegar, mustard seeds, salt, and pepper. Mix well and serve at room temperature.

8 large, juicy
oranges

2 sweet
pineapples

1½ cups
sugar

serves 12

caramelized orange and pineapple

If you can find really sweet pineapples, you won't need
to remove the core.

Using a small, sharp knife, cut away and discard the skin and pith
from the oranges, leaving just the flesh. Cut the oranges in half
lengthwise, then crosswise into slices.

Using a serrated knife, cut off the pineapple skin in strips, working
from the top down and making sure all the little prickly black spots
are removed from the flesh. Cut the pineapples into wedges
lengthwise and remove the cores. If the pineapple is large, cut it
into chunks. Arrange the orange and pineapple on a serving dish.

Put the sugar into a saucepan, heat gently until melted and bubbling,
then cook until golden brown. Remove from the heat and add
¼ cup water—take care, because the mixture will spatter. Stir until
smooth, let cool for 5 minutes, then pour over the prepared fruit.

Note If you want to make a stunning centerpiece, try your hand at
sugar-pulling. Leave a little of the sauce in the pan and, using a
fork, dip into the sauce and then pull away, making long strands of
sugar. Pile these on top of the fruit like a golden cobweb. The
secret of sugar-pulling is the temperature of the sugar—if it runs off
the fork it is too hot, so let it cool. If it is brittle and just snaps when
pulled, it is too cool, so heat it carefully over a very low heat, until
it is flexible. Take care not to overheat the sugar or it will burn.

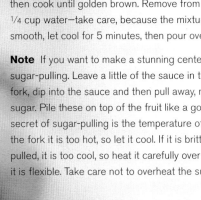

ricepaper packages with dipping soy

These are time-consuming but worth it, so enlist some help when assembling just before the party. Keep them chilled, covered with a damp cloth and plastic wrap, until needed.

12 ricepaper wrappers*	1 tablespoon toasted sesame seeds
2 carrots, cut into matchsticks	
6 scallions, cut into matchsticks	**DIPPING SOY**
4 oz. bean sprouts, 1 cup	2 tablespoons honey
leaves from a bunch of Thai basil	1 tablespoon soy sauce
	1 tablespoon teriyaki sauce
a bunch of watercress	1 red chile, finely sliced

serves 12

Soak the ricepaper wrappers in several changes of warm water until soft, about 4 minutes.

Gather up little clusters of the carrots, scallions, bean sprouts, basil, and watercress and put in the middle of the softened wrappers. Sprinkle with sesame seeds and roll up to enclose the vegetables.

To make the dipping soy, put the honey, soy sauce, and teriyaki sauce into a small bowl and mix. Add the chile and transfer to a small, shallow dish to serve with the packages.

*Note Thai or Vietnamese dried ricepaper wrappers (*bánh tráng*) are sold in Asian markets. Sold in packages of 50–100, they keep well in a cool pantry.

cocktails and finger food

> **THE MENU**
> **FOR 12 PEOPLE**
>
> **Ricepaper Packages with Dipping Soy**
>
> **Smoked Oyster and Goat Cheese Pastries**
>
> **Grissini with Prosciutto**
>
> **Parmesan and Rosemary Wafers**
>
> **Artichoke and Tomato Bread Puffs**
>
> **Raw Vegetable Platter**
>
> **TO DRINK**
> **Cocktails (page 142)**

the scene

It's never worth having a cocktail party for fewer than 12, and they are even better with more. It's a great way to see all your friends, but it is important to serve good drinks and delicious food. I can't bear it when you go to a party and are served supermarket food and sad drinks in plastic glasses. If you don't have enough glasses, rent them from a local wine merchant.

the style

It's important to think about space, so there is room for people to wander and mingle—choose a large room and move the furniture to the edges. I love serving different drinks, so use an assortment of glasses—it adds glamour, too. Decorate the table with leaves, herbs, strips of fabric, and ribbons. Have a few trays handy—you can load one side with nibbles and collect glasses on the other side as you move around the room.

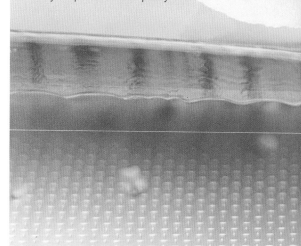

8 oz. puff pastry dough

4 oz. soft goat cheese, crumbled

2 cans smoked oysters, 3 oz. each

1 egg, beaten

sea salt and freshly ground black pepper

a baking tray, buttered

serves 12

smoked oyster and goat cheese pastries

I love smoked oysters and I don't think that enough people know about them, so make these little pastries and let everyone enjoy.

Roll out the dough on a lightly floured surface until very thin, to make a rectangle, then cut in half lengthwise. Put half the crumbled goat cheese down the middle of one piece of dough. Arrange half the oysters in a row on top of the goat cheese. Brush the beaten egg along both the long sides, fold the dough over lengthwise, and gently press the edges together to seal. Repeat with the other piece of dough and remaining cheese and oysters. Lightly brush both puff pastry packages with beaten egg, then sprinkle with salt and pepper. Cut into 1-inch slices, transfer to the prepared baking tray, and cook in a preheated oven at 400°F for 12 minutes until puffed and golden. Let cool to room temperature before serving.

139

grissini with prosciutto

It's best to shop for these ingredients at an Italian gourmet store, as the grissini will be skinny and crunchy, made with good flour in the traditional way, and the prosciutto can be sliced to order. Assemble these up to an hour in advance.

12 very thin slices prosciutto
12 grissini

serves 12

Trim off excess fat from the prosciutto, wrap a slice around each grissini to half the way down, arrange in glasses or on a large plate, and serve.

THE WORK PLAN

the day before

- Make the Parmesan and rosemary wafers.

on the day

- Make the smoked oyster and goat cheese pastries.
- Make the artichoke and bread puffs, but only cook for about 8–10 minutes (finish in oven for 5 minutes just before serving).
- Prepare all the fillings for the ricepaper packages, put into plastic bags with damp paper towels, and chill in the refrigerator.

just before serving

- Assemble the ricepaper packages, arrange on serving dishes.
- Wrap the prosciutto around the grissini and arrange in a glass.
- Chop the raw vegetables and arrange on plates.
- Prepare all the cocktails.

parmesan and rosemary wafers

These are a must for any good party, as the crispness of the cheese is wonderful and the infusion of the rosemary divine. Everyone will be constantly nibbling, so make lots. They can be prepared in advance but must be kept chilled in an airtight container.

2 sprigs of rosemary, leaves stripped and finely chopped

8 oz. Parmesan cheese, coarsely grated

2 baking trays, lined with parchment paper

makes 24

Put the rosemary into a bowl and stir in the Parmesan. Put teaspoons of the mixture in little heaps on the baking trays and flatten out into circles, making sure that they are not too close, as they will spread. Bake in a preheated oven at 400°F for about 8–10 minutes until golden, remove and let cool. Gently peel off the paper and serve.

artichoke and tomato bread puffs

Most supermarkets sell cardboard tubes of croissant or bread dough: both of these work well. Again, enlist some help to put these together, as many hands make light work!

10 oz. ready-made bread dough (*petit pain*)

10 oz. baby artichoke hearts preserved in olive oil

4 oz. mozzarella cheese

24 cherry tomatoes, halved

6 scallions, each cut into 8

sea salt and freshly ground black pepper

2 baking trays, buttered

serves 12

Divide the bread dough into 4, then each again into 12, making 48. Roll out each piece or flatten with the palm of your hand into a disk. Transfer to the baking trays. Drain the artichokes, reserving the oil, and chop to make 48 pieces. Cut the mozzarella into 1/4-inch cubes—you should have 48 pieces.

Arrange a piece of artichoke and one of each of the remaining ingredients on top of each piece of dough, pushing them lightly into the dough to secure them. Sprinkle with a little of the reserved artichoke oil, salt, and pepper. Cook in a preheated oven at 350°F for 12–15 minutes until golden and cooked. Serve hot, warm, or at room temperature.

raw vegetable platter

8 carrots, cut into batons

8 baby fennel bulbs, trimmed and halved

1 cucumber, cut into batons

2 bunches of radishes, trimmed

1/2 cup extra virgin olive oil

3 tablespoons balsamic vinegar

serves 12

Arrange the raw vegetables on a big serving plate. Mix the oil and vinegar in a small dipping bowl and serve with the vegetables.

cocktails

white wine fizz

1 bottle white wine, 750 ml

1 quart sparkling water

1 apple, sliced

1 lemon, sliced

1 orange, sliced

1 kiwifruit, sliced

ice cubes

serves 8

Put all the ingredients into
a pitcher, mix, and serve.

cosmopolitan

8 shots of vodka

3 cups cranberry juice

freshly squeezed juice of 4 limes

ice cubes

serves 8

Put all the ingredients into a pitcher and mix. Alternatively, pour the cranberry juice into individual glasses and top with the vodka and lime.

brown cow

1/2 bottle Kahlua, 350 ml

1 quart milk

ice cubes

serves 8

Put all the ingredients into a pitcher and mix. Alternatively, put the Kahlua into individual glasses, and top with milk and ice.

luscious and lavish dinner

the scene

Pull out all the stops with this luxury menu. It includes lots of things you've always wanted to make, but never known how—or perhaps even that you could! Well, now is your chance to impress your friends.

the style

Simple and pure, with a magnificent table set with elegant white china to show off the magic of this menu. This is the time to use place cards, and it's definitely the time to enlist an extra pair of hands in the kitchen.

THE MENU

FOR 8 PEOPLE

Smoked Wild Salmon and Scrambled Eggs with "Caviar"

Watercress Soup

Beef en Croûte

Mustard Sauce

Seasonal Cheese and Green Leaf Salad

Raspberries in Champagne Gelatin

TO DRINK

Rosé with the Scrambled Egg

Sauvignon Blanc or Chenin Blanc with the Soup

Cabernet Sauvignon with the Beef and Cheese

Late Harvest Sweet Wine with the Gelatin

Reserve Brandy and Coffee

THE WORK PLAN

the day before

- Prepare the beef, wrap it in dough, cover, and chill.
- Make the mustard sauce and chill.

on the day

- Make the champagne gelatin.
- Wash and dry the salad leaves, put into a plastic bag, and chill.
- Remove the cheese from the refrigerator 2 hours in advance, cover with a clean dish cloth.

just before serving

- Cook the beef.
- Make the soup.
- Warm the bread and make the scrambled eggs.
- Reheat the mustard sauce and toss the salad.

smoked wild salmon and scrambled eggs with "caviar"

Use caviar if you are wildly rich—and try the scrambled eggs made with duck eggs. These are available from some gourmet stores and farm shops.

Break the eggs into a bowl and beat lightly. Add the milk and beat again. Melt the butter in a nonstick saucepan, then add the eggs, salt, and pepper. Cook, stirring constantly with a wooden spoon, for 5–8 minutes, until softly scrambled. Remove from the heat just before the eggs are done, as they will carry on cooking off the heat.

Warm the bread in a preheated oven at 350°F for 10 minutes and put onto serving plates. Spoon the scrambled eggs onto the toast and top with smoked salmon. Add a teaspoon of caviar, if using, and serve at once, topped with a few chives.

8 hen eggs
or 4 duck eggs

1/2 cup milk

4 tablespoons
butter

8 slices whole
wheat bread

8 oz. smoked
salmon

3 oz. caviar or
salmon caviar
(optional)

sea salt and
white pepper

a bunch of chives,
to serve

serves 8

watercress soup

My green passion is watercress. I love the fresh crunch that releases a subtle peppery taste—such a palate cleanser. Buy it in bunches, with long stems, an abundance of flawless dark green leaves, and a clean fresh smell. Store in the refrigerator, wrapped in damp newspaper or paper towels, for up to 2 days.

serves 8

Heat the oil in a large saucepan and add the onion, leek, and potatoes. Cook for 15 minutes until soft and translucent. Add the flour, mix well, then add the stock and season with salt and pepper. Heat to simmering and cook for 30 minutes. Using a stick blender, process until smooth. Add the watercress and parsley and simmer for

2 tablespoons
olive oil

1 onion, chopped

1 leek, chopped

2 large potatoes,
cut into even
pieces

2 teaspoons
all-purpose flour

6 cups chicken or
vegetable stock

10 oz. watercress,
stalks removed
and leaves
chopped

a bunch of
flat-leaf parsley,
chopped

sea salt and
freshly ground
black pepper

1/4 cup olive oil

3 shallots, finely chopped

2 garlic cloves, chopped

6 oz. portobello
mushrooms, sliced

3 1/2 lb. beef tenderloin,
trimmed

1 lb. puff or shortcrust
pastry dough

2 eggs, beaten

sea salt and freshly ground
black pepper

serves 8

beef en croûte

For added luxury, use a mixture of porcini and portobello mushrooms. Just make sure they are completely cold when you put them onto the dough, and drain off any excess liquid.

Put 2 tablespoons of the oil into a skillet, heat gently, then add the shallots, garlic, and mushrooms. Cook for 15 minutes, stirring frequently, until soft but not browned and all the liquid has evaporated. Season with salt and pepper, let cool, then chill.

Put 1 tablespoon of the remaining oil into a roasting pan and put into a preheated oven at 425°F for 5 minutes. Rub the tenderloin all over with the remaining oil and salt and pepper, and transfer to the preheated roasting pan. Cook for 15 minutes, then remove. Transfer the beef to a plate, reserving the meat juices for the mustard sauce, and let cool until completely cold. (At this stage, you can make the mustard sauce in the roasting pan and reheat it when you need it.)

Roll out the dough to a rectangle large enough to wrap around the beef. Brush lightly with the beaten eggs. Spoon the mushroom mixture evenly over the dough, leaving a 2-inch border all around. Put the cold beef in the middle of the dough, on top of the mushrooms, and either roll the dough

around the beef or wrap, as if covering a package. Try not to have too much dough at the ends, and trim to avoid areas of double dough. Turn the package so that the seam is underneath, and transfer to a lightly oiled baking tray. Brush all over with the beaten eggs and chill for 2 hours.

Cook on the middle shelf of a preheated oven at 400°F for 20 minutes. Reduce the oven heat to 350°F and continue cooking for 15 minutes for rare, 35 minutes for medium, and 50 minutes for well done. If you are cooking to well done, you may need to reduce the oven temperature to prevent the dough from burning while the beef cooks through.

mustard sauce

This sauce is rather delicious but also rich, so a little goes a long way. If you are making it in advance, after roasting the beef, make it in the roasting pan.

2 tablespoons smooth
Dijon mustard

2 tablespoons
whole-grain mustard

1/2 cup white wine

1 3/4 cups heavy cream

reserved juices from
roasting the beef

serves 8

Put the mustards, white wine, cream, and roasting juices into a saucepan. Bring to a boil, then simmer for 5 minutes. Serve hot with the beef.

seasonal cheese and green leaf salad

My favorite cheese is Vacherin–if ever a cheese was made in heaven, this is it. It comes from Switzerland and the best time to buy is October–November when the milk used to make the cheese has come from cows fed on spring and summer meadow grass. Choose whatever fresh, creamy cheese is available where you live. If you store cheese in the refrigerator, always remove it to room temperature 2 hours before serving.

8 oz. mizuna or other small salad leaves

8 oz. arugula

1 head of escarole, leaves separated

2 tablespoons smooth Dijon mustard

1/3 cup red wine vinegar

3/4 cup olive oil

1–2 cheeses, depending on variety and size

sea salt and freshly ground black pepper

bread or cheese crackers, to serve

serves 8

Wash the mizuna, arugula, and escarole in a lots of cold water. Use a salad spinner to dry all the leaves. Put the mustard and vinegar into a bottle with a secure lid and shake well. Add the olive oil, with salt and pepper to taste, and shake vigorously. Transfer the dry leaves to a large salad bowl and, just before serving, add the dressing. Toss well to coat. Serve the salad with the cheese and bread or crackers.

raspberries in champagne gelatin

This simple but delicious combination is a refreshingly light way to round off an otherwise quite rich menu. If champagne seems a bit decadent, use a good bottle of cava or an American sparkling wine.

2 envelopes powdered gelatin, 1/2 oz. each, or 2 tablespoons

1 lb. raspberries, about 3 cups

1 bottle champagne, at room temperature

8 glasses

serves 8

Put 3 tablespoons hot water into a small bowl and sprinkle in the gelatin. Set aside in a warm place to dissolve, about 10 minutes. Divide the raspberries between the glasses. Open the champagne and add a little to the dissolved gelatin. Transfer to a pitcher and add the remaining champagne. Mix gently so that you don't build up a froth. Pour into the glasses on top of the raspberries and chill for 2 hours, until set.

the scene

This menu makes a welcome change after all that traditional Christmas food. The seafood lasagne is light and elegant, but also luxurious, and can be made in advance and reheated.

the style

Cover the table with rich colors and have plenty of candles to match the Christmas tree lights. Wrap a little gift for every guest, to carry on the tradition and spirit of giving into the New Year.

THE MENU

FOR 12 PEOPLE

Beet, Goat Cheese, and Pine Nut Salad with Melba Toast

Seafood Lasagne

Dry-Fry Chile Greens

Raspberry and Chocolate Tart

TO DRINK

Gamay with the Salad

Sauvignon Blanc or Chenin Blanc with the Lasagne

Muscat or Sauternes with the Tart

new year's eve dinner

THE WORK PLAN

the day before

- Make the seafood lasagne, cover, and chill.
- Make and cook chocolate base for the tart.

on the day

- Make the Melba toast. Store in an airtight container.
- Roast the beets, cool, and peel.
- Make the salad dressing.
- Prepare the greens.
- Assemble the chocolate tart and freeze. (Remove from freezer 30 minutes before serving.)

just before serving

- Reheat the lasagne in a preheated oven at 350°F for 30 minutes, reduce to 300°F, and cook for 30 minutes.
- Assemble the salad.
- Dress the salad.
- Cook the greens.

beet, goat cheese, and pine nut salad with melba toast

Wintry, festive sumptuousness, thanks to the deep red of the beets and the bright white of the cheese.

12 slices white, sliced bread

1¹⁄₂ lb. small unpeeled beets, trimmed

1 lb. mixed leaves

8 oz. crumbly goat cheese

4 oz. pine nuts, toasted in a dry skillet

a bunch of basil

2 garlic cloves, crushed and chopped

¹⁄₂ cup olive oil

freshly squeezed juice of 2 lemons

salt and freshly ground black pepper

serves 12

To make the Melba toast, toast the slices of bread, then remove the crusts. Using a large, sharp knife, split each piece of toast through the middle, to give 2 whole slices of toast with 1 soft bread side each. Cut in half diagonally, then cook under a preheated broiler, soft side up, until golden and curled. Watch the toasts carefully, as they can burn quickly.

Put the beets into a roasting pan and roast in a preheated oven at 350°F for 45 minutes. Remove, let cool, then peel and quarter. Put the mixed leaves onto a big serving dish, add the beets, crumble the goat cheese on top, then sprinkle with pine nuts and torn basil leaves.

Put the garlic, oil, and lemon juice into a small bowl or jar. Add salt and pepper, mix well, then pour over the salad and serve with the Melba toast.

seafood lasagne

This dish can be prepared completely in advance, leaving you free to enjoy yourself—yet it is still special enough to serve on a big occasion. Choose from shrimp, mussels, oysters, crab, lobster, clams, salmon, trout, cod, haddock, tuna, marlin, swordfish, shrimp, and scallops. Have a mixture of just four of these fish or seafood and savor the individual flavors. Choose according to your budget and availability and ask your fish seller for advice. Anything in a shell, such as mussels or clams, should be removed from the shell and all large pieces of fish should be skinned, boned, and cut into even pieces. Make sure you dry all the fish and seafood thoroughly with paper towels.

1/4 cup olive oil

2 sticks butter

2 garlic cloves, chopped

1 onion, chopped

1 fennel bulb, trimmed and chopped

2 leeks, sliced

2/3 cup all-purpose flour

1 1/4 cups fish stock

2 cups white wine

2 lb. mixed seafood (see recipe introduction), rinsed and dried

a large bunch of flat-leaf parsley, finely chopped

3/4 cup heavy cream

1 lb. dried lasagne pasta

8 oz. Parmesan cheese, freshly grated

sea salt and freshly ground black pepper

a lasagne or roasting dish, about 12 x 8 inches

serves 12

Put the oil and 4 tablespoons of the butter into a large saucepan and heat well. Add the garlic, onion, fennel, and leeks and cook for 10 minutes, stirring frequently, until soft and translucent. Using a sifter, sprinkle 3 tablespoons of the flour in a thin layer over the top. Mix with a wooden spoon to absorb the excess oil and cook for a few minutes. Gradually add the fish stock and 1/2 cup of the wine, stirring constantly to form a smooth sauce.

Add the prepared seafood and parsley to the sauce with salt and pepper to taste. Gently mix and simmer over low heat for 5 minutes. Remove from the heat and set aside.

Heat the remaining butter in another saucepan, add the remaining flour, and stir until smooth. Cook for a few minutes, then remove from the heat and slowly add the remaining wine, stirring with a wire whisk. When all the wine has been added, return the saucepan to the heat, bring to a boil, and simmer for 2 minutes. Add the cream, salt, and pepper, then remove from the heat.

Put a layer of the prepared seafood into the lasagne dish, pour over some sauce and top with a layer of lasagne. Repeat until the dish is full and all the seafood, sauce, and lasagne have been used. Top with the Parmesan and chill until needed.

Bake in a preheated oven at 350°F for 50 minutes until bubbling and golden.

dry-fry chile greens

I know this is a last minute dish, but really it is so easy that it won't put you under pressure and the result is just delicious, especially with the seafood lasagne. For the greens, use a selection of curly kale, Savoy cabbage, red chard, or other greens.

1 tablespoon vegetable oil

2 tablespoons butter

1 lb. greens, coarsely chopped

½ teaspoon hot red pepper flakes

zest and juice of 2 unwaxed lemons

freshly ground black pepper

serves 12

Heat the oil and butter in a wok or large saucepan, add the greens, and cook for 5 minutes, tossing frequently. Add the pepper flakes, lemon zest, and juice. Cook for a further minute and transfer to a serving dish. Sprinkle with pepper and serve.

raspberry and chocolate tart

2 sticks butter

7 squares (7 oz.) bittersweet chocolate

4 eggs

1 cup sugar

1 cup ground almonds, or 1¼ cups slivered almonds ground in a food processor

1⅓ cups self-rising flour

14 oz. raspberries, about 2½ cups

1 lb. raspberry yogurt ice cream

a springform cake pan, 10 inches diameter, buttered

serves 12

Put the butter and chocolate into a saucepan and melt gently over very low heat. Put the eggs and sugar into a bowl and beat, using an electric beater, for 6 minutes until stiff and creamy. Pour the melted chocolate into the eggs and sugar and continue beating until mixed. Using a large metal spoon, fold in the ground almonds and flour. Pour the mixture into the prepared cake pan and top with about one third of the raspberries.

Bake in a preheated oven at 350°F for 30–40 minutes until set, then remove and let cool in the pan. When cool, turn out the cake onto a plate. Pile the ice cream on top, then push the remaining raspberries into the ice cream. Transfer to the freezer for up to 2 hours, but remove 20 minutes before serving.

index

conversion charts

Weights and measures have been rounded up or down slightly to make measuring easier.

VOLUME EQUIVALENTS

american	metric	imperial
1 teaspoon	5 ml	
1 tablespoon	15 ml	
1/4 cup	60 ml	2 fl.oz.
1/3 cup	75 ml	2 1/2 fl.oz.
1/2 cup	125 ml	4 fl.oz.
2/3 cup	150 ml	5 fl.oz. (1/4 pint)
3/4 cup	175 ml	6 fl.oz.
1 cup	250 ml	8 fl.oz.

WEIGHT EQUIVALENTS

imperial	metric
1 oz.	25 g
2 oz.	50 g
3 oz.	75 g
4 oz.	125 g
5 oz.	150 g
6 oz.	175 g
7 oz.	200 g
8 oz. (1/2 lb.)	250 g
9 oz.	275 g
10 oz.	300 g
11 oz.	325 g
12 oz.	375 g
13 oz.	400 g
14 oz.	425 g
15 oz.	475 g
16 oz. (1 lb.)	500 g
2 1b.	1 kg

MEASUREMENTS:

inches	cm
1/4 inch	5 mm
1/2 inch	1 cm
3/4 inch	1.5 cm
1 inch	2.5 cm
2 inches	5 cm
3 inches	7 cm
4 inches	10 cm
5 inches	12 cm
6 inches	15 cm
7 inches	18 cm
8 inches	20 cm
9 inches	23 cm
10 inches	25 cm
11 inches	28 cm
12 inches	30 cm

OVEN TEMPERATURES:

225°F	110°C	Gas 1/4
250°F	120°C	Gas 1/2
275°F	140°C	Gas 1
300°F	150°C	Gas 2
325°F	160°C	Gas 3
350°F	180°C	Gas 4
375°F	190°C	Gas 5
400°F	200°C	Gas 6
425°F	220°C	Gas 7
450°F	230°C	Gas 8
475°F	240°C	Gas 9

Publisher's Acknowledgements

The publisher would like to thank everyone who allowed us to photograph in their homes, including Vanessa Arbuthnott, Ivan Barge and Heather Murphy, Stephan Schulte, and Julie and Mark O'Shaughnessy. Thanks also to Graham Philips, architect of Skywood House, Middlesex. "Seascape" The Beach House (pages 124–131) is available for film and photo shoots at 20 The Suttons, Camber, East Sussex TN31 YSA, UK. Telephone 00 44 1797 224 754, email. sea-scape@cwcom.net, www.seascape.cwc.net/seascape.htm.

Author's Acknowledgements

From the top: Debi Treloar for the most delicious photographs, kindest heart, my working mother soul mate. Sally Somers for all her cooking, eating, and, best of all for me, the hardest working editor, and the maddest sense of humour—always a laugh. The ever-calm and hardworking Viki Keppel Compton, my assistant, who managed to buy a boat and sail away for 6 weeks—yes we were jealous, but you did come back. Thanks for all that cooking, testing, and washing up. Emily Chalmers, who scoured the shelves and stores to search out my ever-exacting requests for dishes, bowls, and cooking utensils—have a great wedding from us all. Paul, who had to put up with all us girls, and create this book out of a wealth of perfect photographs. Thanks for the thoughtful and beautiful Lina Ikse Bergman, Debi's ever-endearing assistant who, every day smiles, helps everyone, and adds a magic bubbliness to the day—we all love you.

Alison Starling for introducing me to RPS and asking me to do another book. Gabriella Le Grazie for getting us all together and keeping that watchful eye on the progress. Elsa Petersen-Schepelern for her gentle input, which allows all the RPS books to be so individual to each author. Kate Brunt for helping to source and come up with some amazing locations. Louise Leffler who started work on the early days of this book—thanks for your input and direction in the south of France. All the owners of the locations who allowed us into their homes, to rearrange their furniture, and put our style into their houses, especially Gerrard and Claire in France, who welcomed us and introduced us to their friend's house—thanks you mad ones!

Very special love and hugs go to all my family, Mum, Dad, brothers, and sister. You helped me do what I do today—thanks. Lastly, masses of thanks to my beloved, who, without his patience, gentle kindness, help with the children, and talent as a great listener, none of this would ever be possible. I love you David.